Georgia

THE THIRTEEN COLONIES

Georgia

CRAIG A. DOHERTY

KATHERINE M. DOHERTY

Facts On File, Inc.

Georgia

Copyright © 2005 by Craig A. Doherty and Katherine M. Doherty

Maps and graph copyright © 2005 by Facts On File, Inc.
Captions copyright © 2005 by Facts On File, Inc.

All rights reserved. No part of this book may be reproduced or utilized in any form or by any means, electronic or mechanical, including photocopying, recording, or by any information storage or retrieval systems, without permission in writing from the publisher. For information contact:

Facts On File, Inc.
132 West 31st Street
New York NY 10001

Library of Congress Cataloging-in-Publication Data
Doherty, Craig A.
   Georgia / Craig A. Doherty and Katherine M. Doherty.
     p. cm. — (The thirteen colonies)
   Includes bibliographical references and index.
   ISBN 0-8160-5419-3
   1. Georgia—History—Colonial period, ca. 1600–1775—Juvenile literature. 2. Georgia—History—1775–1865—Juvenile literature. I. Doherty, Katherine M. II. Title.
   F289.D64 2006
   975.8'02—dc22   2005001891

Facts On File books are available at special discounts when purchased in bulk quantities for businesses, associations, institutions or sales promotions. Please call our Special Sales Department in New York at (212) 967-8800 or (800) 322-8755.

You can find Facts On File on the World Wide Web at http://www.factsonfile.com

Text design by Erika K. Arroyo
Cover design by Semadar Megged
Maps and graph by Sholto Ainslie

Printed in the United States of America

VB FOF 10 9 8 7 6 5 4 3 2 1

This book is printed on acid-free paper.

Note on Photos

Many of the illustrations and photographs used in this book are old, historical images. The quality of the prints is not always up to current standards, as in some cases the originals are from old or poor-quality negatives or are damaged. The content of the illustrations, however, made their inclusion important despite problems in reproduction.

This book is dedicated to
the many students of all ages
we have worked with and taught over the years.

Contents

Introduction	xiii
Map: The Thirteen Colonies, 1790	xviii
1 First Contacts	**1**
Conflicting Claims	1
Map: Land Claimed by Spain in North America, 16th Century	3
Native Americans in Georgia	4
Map: Native Americans of Georgia	5
CORN	8
CREEK GAMES	11
2 The Spanish and French in Georgia	**16**
HUGUENOTS	16
PIRATES, PRIVATEERS, AND SPANISH TREASURE	19
Conflict between the Spanish and the English over Georgia	25
DR. HENRY WOODWARD (CA. 1646–1686)	26
THE MARGRAVATE OF AZILIA	28
3 The English Colony of Georgia	**31**
JAMES EDWARD OGLETHORPE (CA. 1696–1785)	34

Silk	35
Oglethorpe and the Colonists Arrive in Georgia	36
Laying Out Savannah	39
City Planning	40
The Diseases Faced by the Colonists in Georgia	43

4 Life in Colonial Georgia — 46

Graph: Population Growth in Georgia, 1740–1790	46
Early Settlers and Settlements in Georgia	47
The Methodist Church	50
Indentured Servants	52
Slavery in Georgia	53
Slavery	55
The War of Jenkins' Ear	57
Jenkins' Ear	59

5 The Royal Colony of Georgia — 63

Mary Musgrove Matthews Bosomworth (ca. 1700–1763)	65
Royal Government	66
The French and Indian Wars (ca. 1689–1762)	68
Map: Treaty of Augusta, November 10, 1763	70

6 The Road to Revolution — 72

Loyalists versus Patriots	73
The Stamp Act (March 22, 1765)	75

THE SONS OF LIBERTY	76
THE STAMP ACT CONGRESS (OCTOBER 1766)	77
The Townshend Duties (June 29, 1767)	79
The Tea Act (May 10, 1773)	82
The Intolerable Acts (1774)	83
LIBERTY POLES AND TREES	84
The First Continental Congress (1774)	85

7 The War for Independence — 87

The War Starts in the North	87
Georgia Joins the Revolution	89
GEORGIA DELEGATES ELECTED TO THE SECOND CONTINENTAL CONGRESS (JULY 1775)	90
DECLARING INDEPENDENCE (1776)	91
The War Comes to Georgia	94
NANCY HART	96

8 Building a Nation — 99

The Articles of Confederation	101
The Constitutional Convention (1787)	104
PREAMBLE TO THE U.S. CONSTITUTION	106
The Fourth State	106

Georgia Time Line	**109**
Georgia Historical Sites	**112**
Further Reading	**116**
Books	116
Web Sites	116
Index	**117**

Introduction

In the 11th century, Vikings from Scandinavia sailed to North America. They explored the Atlantic coast and set up a few small settlements. In Newfoundland and Nova Scotia, Canada, archaeologists have found traces of these settlements. No one knows for sure why they did not establish permanent colonies. It may have been that it was too far away from their homeland. At about the same time, many Scandinavians were involved with raiding and establishing settlements along the coasts of what are now Great Britain and France. This may have offered greater rewards than traveling all the way to North America.

When the western part of the Roman Empire fell in 476, Europe lapsed into a period of almost 1,000 years of war, plague, and hardship. This period of European history is often referred to as the Dark Ages or Middle Ages. Communication between the different parts of Europe was almost nonexistent. If other Europeans knew about the Vikings' explorations westward, they left no record of it. Between the time of Viking exploration and Christopher Columbus's 1492 journey, Europe underwent many changes.

By the 15th century, Europe had experienced many advances. Trade within the area and with the Far East had created prosperity for the governments and many wealthy people. The Catholic Church had become a rich and powerful institution. Although wars would be fought and governments would come and go, the countries of Western Europe had become fairly strong. During this time, Europe rediscovered many of the arts and sciences that had

Vikings explored the Atlantic coast of North America in ships similar to this one. *(National Archives of Canada)*

existed before the fall of Rome. They also learned much from their trade with the Near and Far East. Historians refer to this time as the Renaissance, which means "rebirth."

At this time, some members of the Catholic Church did not like the direction the church was going. People such as Martin Luther and John Calvin spoke out against the church. They soon gained a number of followers who decided that they would protest and form their own churches. The members of these new churches were called Protestants. The movement to establish these new churches is called the Protestant Reformation. It would have a big impact on America as many Protestant groups would leave Europe so they could worship the way they wanted to.

In addition to religious dissent, problems arose with the overland trade routes to the Far East. The Ottoman Turks took control of the lands in the Middle East and disrupted trade. It was at this time that European explorers began trying to find a water route to the Far East. The explorers first sailed around Africa. Then an Italian named Christopher Columbus convinced the king and queen of Spain that it would be shorter to sail west to Asia rather than go around Africa. Most sailors and educated people at the time knew the world was round. However, Columbus made two errors in his calculations. First, he did not realize just how big the Earth is, and second, he did not know that the continents of North and South America blocked a westward route to Asia.

When Columbus made landfall in 1492, he believed that he was in the Indies, as the Far East was called at the time. For a period of time after Columbus, the Spanish controlled the seas and the exploration of what was called the New World. England tried to compete with the Spanish on the high seas, but their ships were no match for the floating fortresses of the Spanish Armada. These heavy ships, known as galleons, ruled the Atlantic.

In 1588, that all changed. A fleet of English ships fought a series of battles in which their smaller but faster and more maneuverable ships finally defeated the Spanish Armada. This opened up the New World to anyone willing to cross the ocean. Portugal, Holland, France, and England all funded voyages of exploration to the New World. In North America, the French explored the far north. The Spanish had already established colonies in what are now Florida, most of the Caribbean, and much of Central and South America. The Dutch

Depicted in this painting, Christopher Columbus completed three additional voyages to the Americas after his initial trip in search of a westward route to Asia in 1492. *(Library of Congress, Prints and Photographs Division [LC-USZ62-103980])*

bought Manhattan and would establish what would become New York, as well as various islands in the Caribbean and lands in South America. The English claimed most of the east coast of North America and set about creating colonies in a variety of ways.

Companies were formed in England and given royal charters to set up colonies. Some of the companies sent out military and trade expeditions to find gold and other riches. They employed men such as John Smith, Bartholomew Gosnold, and others to explore the lands they had been granted. Other companies found groups of Protestants who wanted to leave England and worked out deals that let them establish colonies. No matter what circumstances a colony was established under, the first settlers suffered hardships as

After Columbus's exploration of the Americas, the Spanish controlled the seas, largely because of their galleons, or large, heavy ships, that looked much like this model. *(Library of Congress, Prints and Photographs Division [LC-USZ62-103297])*

they tried to build communities in what to them was a wilderness. They also had to deal with the people who were already there.

Native Americans lived in every corner of the Americas. There were vast and complex civilizations in Central and South America. The city that is now known as Cahokia was located along the Mississippi River in what is today Illinois and may have had as many as 50,000 residents. The people of Cahokia built huge earthen mounds that can still be seen today. There has been a lot of speculation as to the total population of Native Americans in 1492. Some have put the number as high as 40 million people.

Most of the early explorers encountered Native Americans. They often wrote descriptions of them for the people of Europe. They also kidnapped a few of these people, took them back to Europe, and put them on display. Despite the number of Native Americans, the Europeans still claimed the land as their own. The rulers of Europe and the Catholic Church at the time felt they had a right to take any lands they wanted from people who did not share their level of technology and who were not Christians.

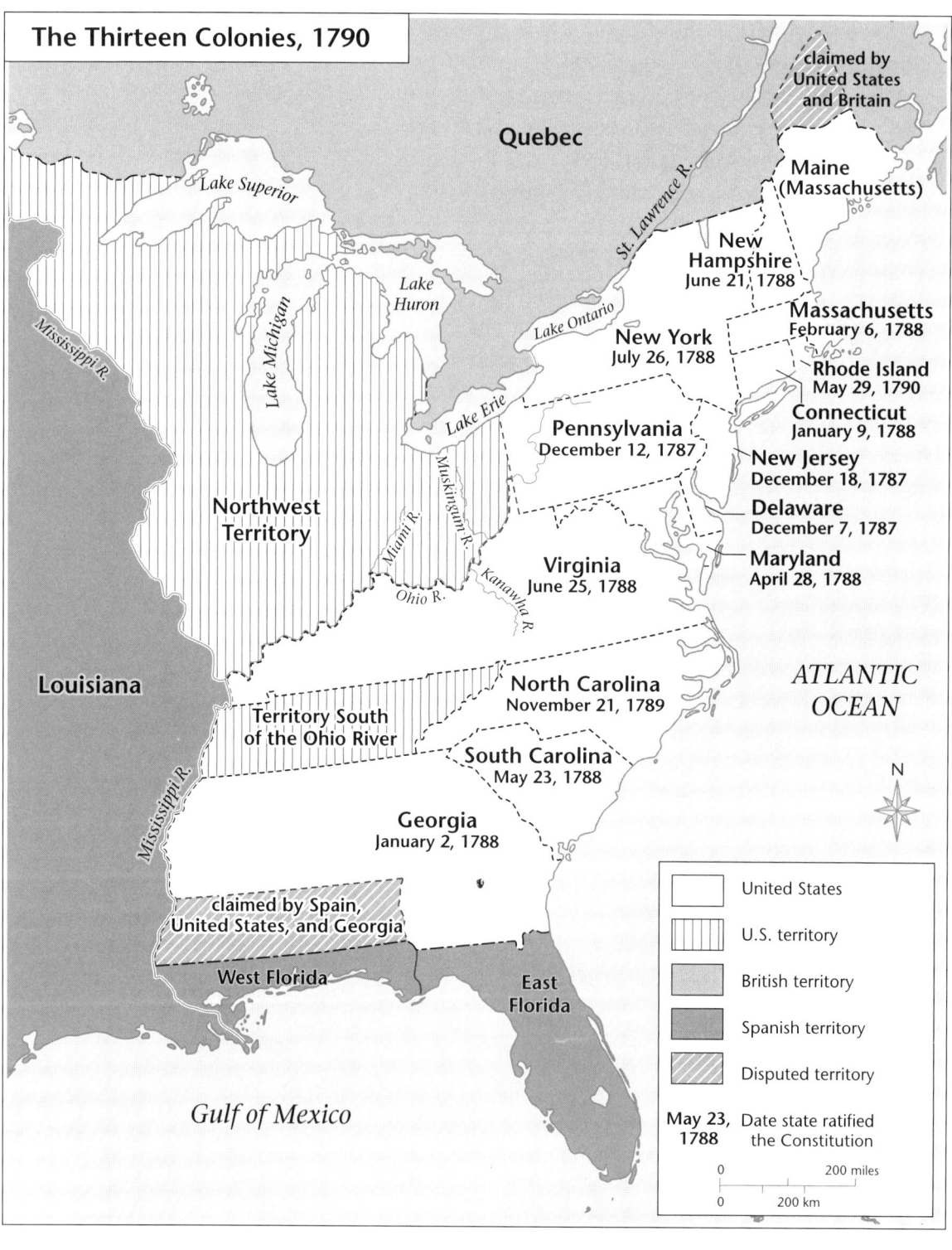

1

First Contacts

CONFLICTING CLAIMS

The land that is now Georgia became an area of conflicting claims among the countries of Europe shortly after Christopher Columbus found his way to the West Indies in 1492. Based on Columbus's voyage, Spain laid claim to most of the Western

In this painting, John Cabot prepares to leave Bristol, England, for North America in his ship *Mathew*. *(National Archives of Canada)*

Hemisphere, and the Spanish were the first to land on the coast of North America and try to settle there. The English also claimed much of the area. John Cabot sailed west from England in 1497 and explored the coast of North America from Greenland south. It is believed that he headed back to England after sailing south to about latitude 38 degrees, somewhere off the Virginia coast.

Although Cabot probably did not get as far south as Georgia, England claimed the territory anyway. At the time, what a country claimed was not as important as what it could settle and defend. As it turned out, claiming the land of what is today Georgia was far easier than creating a colony there. There were a number of attempts to colonize what is now Georgia before the English finally created a colony there in the 1700s.

In addition to the Spanish and English, the French also claimed this same area. In 1525, Giovanni da Verrazano, an Italian sailing for the French, claimed much of North America for France. Over the next 150 years, there were a number of attempts to colonize the area that the Spanish called "Carolana," which in Latin means "land of Charles." Charles I was king of Spain at the time, and the land was named in his honor.

In the early 1500s, the Spanish were successful in establishing a number of colonies on the islands of the Caribbean and in Central and South America. Their colonies depended on the enslavement of the Native American people they encountered there. No one has been able to give an accurate number of the population of Native Americans in 1492. However, the best estimates today suggest that there were far more Native Americans than previously thought. It is now believed that Hispaniola, which is the second-largest island in the Caribbean, may have been home to as many as 8 million Native Americans in 1492. However, slavery and European diseases reduced that number to a few hundred in less than 100 years.

In the 1500s, the Spanish also became interested in the mainland of North America. In May 1539, Hernando de Soto and a

Charles I ruled England, Scotland, and Ireland from 1625 until his execution in 1649. *(Library of Congress, Prints and Photographs Division [LC-USZ62-91631])*

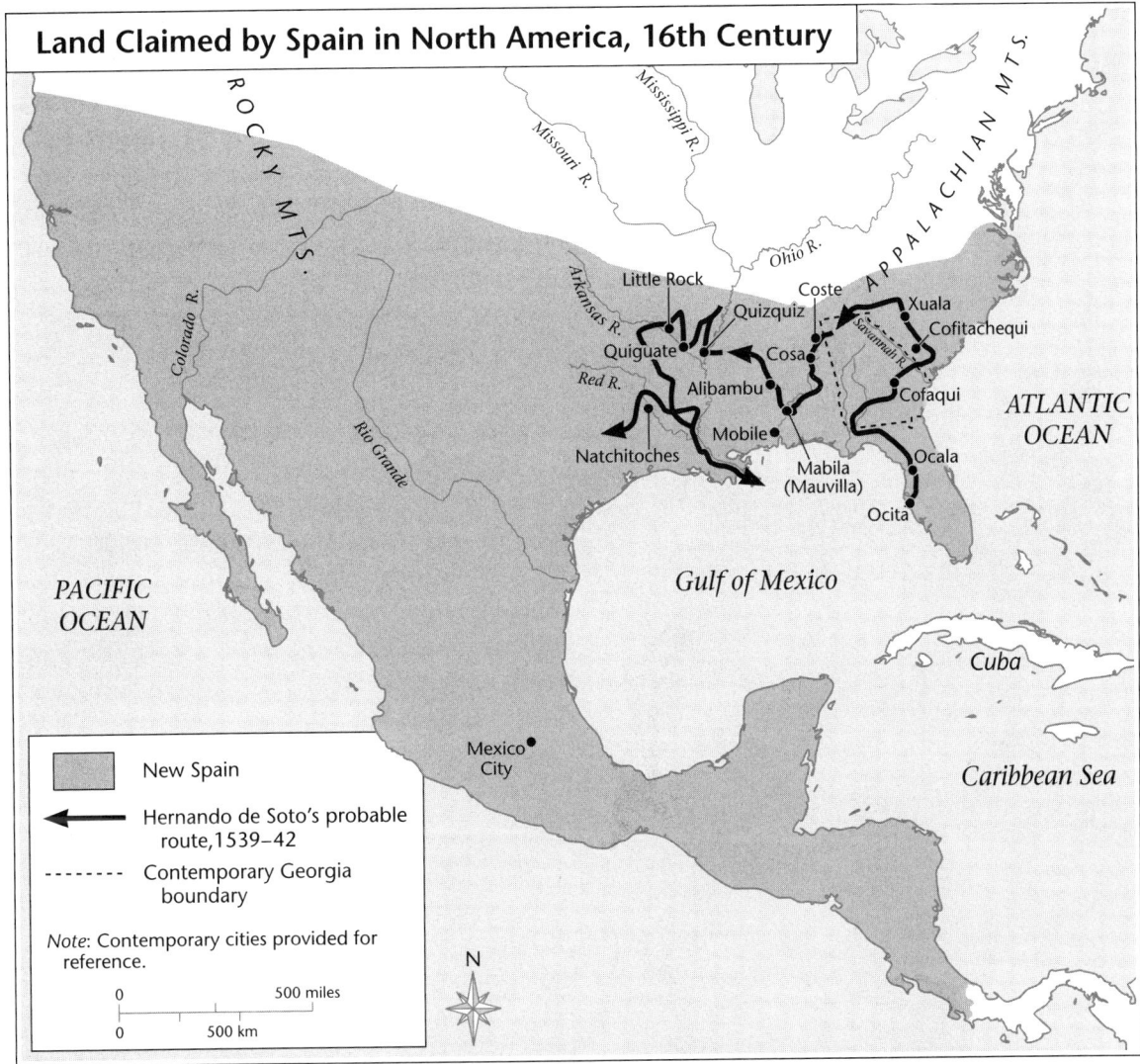

Based on the exploration of Hernando de Soto and others, Spain claimed much of the southern part of North America.

force of 600 men landed near what is now Tampa Bay, Florida. From there, they traveled north along the coast of the Gulf of Mexico. The reports from the time have conflicting details, but it is believed that de Soto and his men traveled throughout what is now the southeastern quarter of the United States, including what are now the states of Florida, Alabama, Georgia, South Carolina, North Carolina, Tennessee, Mississippi, Arkansas, Louisiana, and Texas.

First Contacts

Shown in an illustration published in 1892, Hernando de Soto and a force of 600 people explored what is now the southeastern United States, killing American Indians and destroying their villages as they traveled. *(Library of Congress, Prints and Photographs Division [LC-USZ62-104329])*

De Soto used his small army to take whatever he needed or wanted from the Native Americans whom he met along the way. When the Native Americans resisted, de Soto had his men kill them and burn their villages. De Soto never made it back from his trip. He died of fever on May 21, 1542, near the junctions of the Canadian and Arkansas Rivers in present-day Oklahoma. His men, fearing attacks from Native Americans if they learned that de Soto had died, kept his death a secret. Instead of burying him, de Soto's men weighted his body and slipped it into a river.

At one time, historians wrote about de Soto as a great explorer who helped create interest in settling the southeastern corner of North America. However, today, de Soto is seen as a greedy and despotic explorer who did immense harm to the Native Americans whom he exposed to European diseases and treated brutally. Some of the Native American groups of the lower Mississippi River basin quickly died out from the smallpox epidemic that de Soto left behind. Although de Soto's impact was almost entirely negative, it was significant because he and his men were probably the first Europeans to travel in what is now Georgia. It is known from reports from the survivors of the de Soto expedition and later explorers, missionaries, and colonists that the area was populated by numerous Native Americans who belonged to a number of different tribes.

NATIVE AMERICANS IN GEORGIA

The Native American tribes in the area that would become Georgia included the Cherokee, Chiaha, Creek, Hitchiti, Tamathli, and Yamasee. There may have been as many as 500 different tribes in North America, and they are now classified by scientists in several ways. One way is by what are called culture areas. These are based on the area in which they lived, their culture, and their language. The Indians of Georgia are considered part of the Southeast Culture Area. The other classification is by language group. The

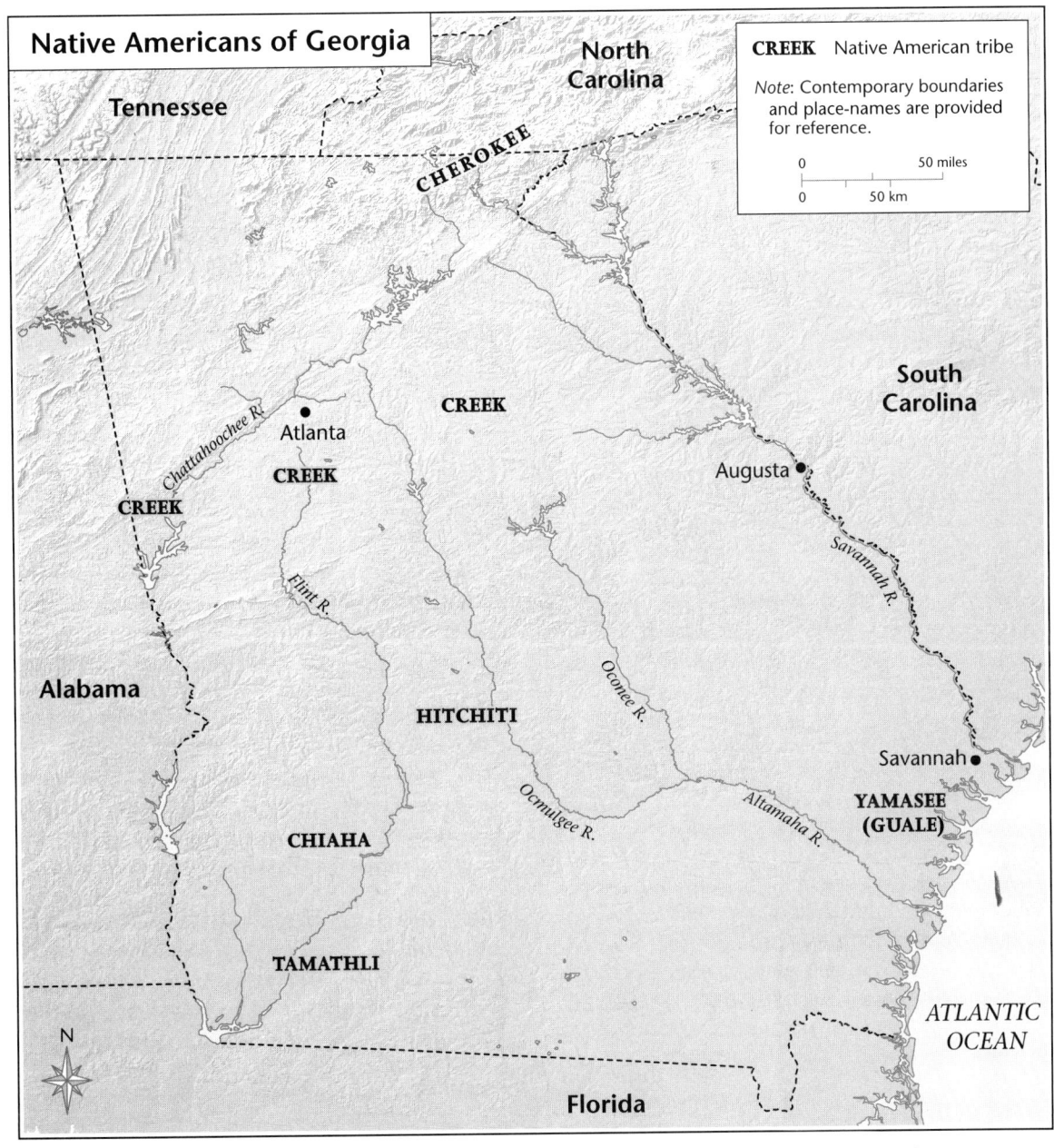

Georgia had been populated for thousands of years prior to the arrival of Europeans. In the 17th century, there were numerous tribes living in the area.

Cherokee, who lived in the Appalachian Mountains from Georgia north to Virginia, spoke a language from the Iroquoian language family. The other tribes in Georgia spoke variations of the Muskogean language.

The Creek, who were the largest and most powerful group of the area, are often referred to as the Muskogee, and the name of the language group is based on this. The name Creek was given to the Muskogee by early English colonists who observed that the tribes almost always built their villages along the many creeks in the area. Archaeologists and anthropologists believe that the Creek are descended from an earlier culture in the Southeast known as the Mound Builders.

Throughout the South and Midwest, especially in the valley of the Mississippi River and its tributaries, starting sometime around 1000 B.C. a number of cultures developed that built a variety of earthen mounds. These mounds tend to come in two forms: pyramid-like mounds that usually had a building on top and earthworks that represented various animals and symbols. The most recent of these mound-building cultures was still in existence when de Soto traveled through the Southeast. There are a number of Mound Builder sites in Georgia, including Etowah, Kolomoki, Hollywood, and Ocmulgee. Most of these mounds are pyramids of different sizes. The largest mound of Etowah is 70 feet high and 380 by 330 feet at the base. These mounds were usually built over long periods of time, as the dirt had to be added a basketful at a time.

Near modern-day Eatonton in central Georgia is the Rock Eagle Mound. This mound is made of rocks arranged in the shape

The Cherokee were one of many Native American tribes that lived in the area that would become Georgia. Austenaco, shown here, was a Cherokee chief during the late 18th century. *(Library of Congress, Prints and Photographs Division [LC-USZ62-90958])*

of a giant eagle. The eagle is 120 feet from the end of one wing to the end of the other wing and 102 feet from the top of its head to the tip of its tail. Scientists have been unable to determine why the Mound Builders created mounds like the Rock Eagle Mound, but they speculate that they had some religious significance.

The Mound Builders of Georgia and elsewhere were farmers who grew corn, beans, squashes, and tobacco in the alluvial soil (the rich soil deposit by the flooding of a river) along the rivers of the area. The largest Mound Builder community was Cahokia in Illinois near modern-day Saint Louis, Missouri, and may have had a

Rock Eagle Mound, located near present-day Eatonton, Georgia, is a large eagle-shaped mound made of rocks. *(Library of Congress, Prints and Photographs Division [HABS, GA, 119-EAT.V,1-1])*

First Contacts

population of more than 30,000 people. At the beginning of the 1500s, many of the Mound Builder sites in the Southeast were still inhabited. Within approximately 100 years, most of the Mound Builder communities had been abandoned. Although there is no way to prove it, many believe that the epidemics of smallpox and other European diseases introduced by the de Soto expedition caused the end of the Mound Builder civilization.

The Creek and other groups who are considered to be the descendants of the Mound Builders continued much of the culture's lifestyle but ended up living in smaller and more scattered communities. The Creek were broken into many subgroups throughout what is now Alabama and Georgia. The Creek are often divided into two main groups: the Upper and Lower Creek. The Upper Creek lived primarily in Alabama, while the Lower Creek were found in Georgia. The way they lived is considered typical of all the tribes in the area.

Corn

One of the greatest American Indian contributions is corn. Around 8,000 B.C., Indians in what is now Mexico began collecting seeds from a native grass plant and cultivating them. Through careful seed selection, they transformed this grass into what is now called corn. By the time Columbus arrived in the Caribbean, the American Indians had developed more than 700 varieties of corn. Different varieties were needed for different purposes and growing conditions.

There are five main types of corn. Popcorn was probably the earliest type that was developed. Its small kernels open when they are heated. Flint corn is similar to popcorn but with bigger kernels and was adapted to grow in northern climates. Flour corn is a variety that can be ground into cornmeal and used to make tortillas or cornbread. Dent corn is a variety that can be ground into meal or used whole in soups and stews. Sweet corn is the type of corn that is usually eaten fresh as corn on the cob.

By the time Columbus arrived in the Caribbean, the cultivation of corn had spread throughout Middle America, the Caribbean, the Southwest, and most of the eastern half of what would become the United States. The cultivation of corn allowed American Indians to stay in one area and establish numerous complex civilizations.

For the Creek, the village was the most important political unit. Each village had a leader known as a *micco*. This person worked much like a modern mayor does. The micco was assisted in running the village by a council of elders. These elders were referred to as the "Beloved Men." The villages were often divided into two "towns." The warriors of the village lived in the "red town" and were responsible for protecting the village and raiding against the village's enemies. Any ceremonies dealing with the warriors took place in the "red town." The other part of the village was known as the "white town." This is where the peaceful members of the tribe lived. They were in charge of any alliances the tribe had and would provide shelter to anyone in need.

At the center of each village was a large round building with walls made of mud and wattle. This is a style of building where a framework of poles and sticks (the wattle) is coated with mud to make a thick solid wall. The roofs of these buildings were often made of bark laid over a wooden framework. The roofs of these buildings were as much as 25 feet high. These central buildings were used as the ceremonial lodges for the village. Older members of the tribe sometimes lived in the ceremonial building. Most Creek villages also had another public building that was used as a meeting place for the micco and the council.

Clustered around the public buildings were the homes of the families in the village. Each family usually had four buildings grouped together. One building served as their winter house; another was their summer house. Of the other two buildings, one was used as a granary to store food, while the other was used as a warehouse for the family's tools and additional belongings.

This engraving by Theodor de Bry based on a painting by John White records the Algonquian village of Secotan, including its crops and homes. The cultivation of crops, such as corn, allowed American Indians to settle in an area. *(Library of Congress, Prints and Photographs Division [LC-USZ62-52444])*

First Contacts

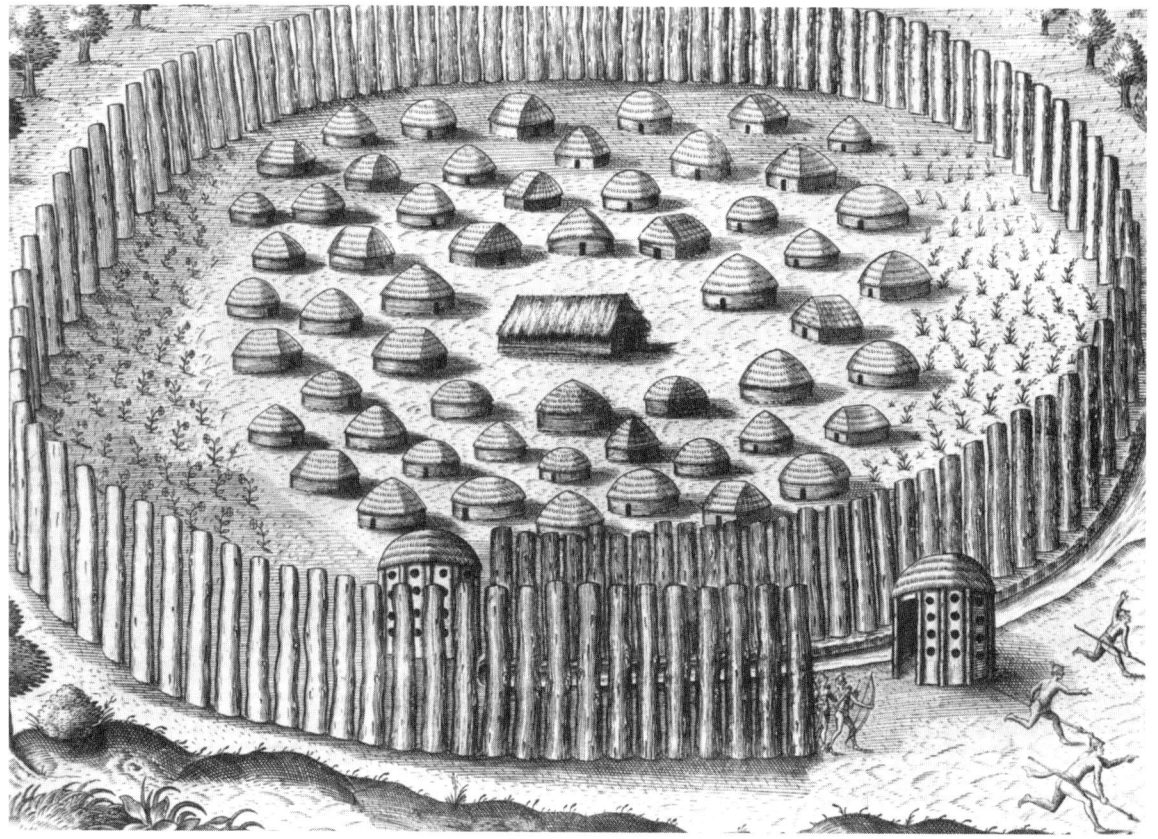

To protect themselves, some tribes built palisades (also called stockades), or a perimeter around their villages made of tall timbers, sharpened at one end and driven into the ground. *(Library of Congress)*

Most of these buildings were made using the same mud and wattle technique as the public buildings. In some cases, the summer houses were built without walls to make a cool, shaded place for the family to work and live.

Often a Creek village was surrounded by a wall known as a palisade. This wall was made of logs stood upright in a ditch. The tops of the logs were sharpened to make it hard to climb over the wall, and the bottoms were buried to make the wall difficult to knock over. The palisade was built to help protect the village from its enemies.

In addition to these public and private buildings, there was also a public square in most Creek villages that had earthen benches built around it. The public square was used for a variety

Creek Games

The Creek, as well as most of the tribes of the Southeast, played a number of games. The two best-known games of the Creek were chunkey and a form of the game that is known today as lacrosse. Chunkey was a game of skill where a round stone disk was rolled down the center of the public square, and the participants tried to hit the disk by throwing spears at it.

The form of lacrosse played by the Indians of the Southeast involved sticks with leather webbing on the end and a deerskin ball. Each team tried to get the ball into the goal of the opposing team. Often teams from different villages competed against each other. The Creek referred to the game as "brother to war," as the players were allowed to hit their opponents with their sticks and even punch them. The most violent form of the game was played by the villages' warriors. The game was sometimes played less violently and included both men and women on the teams.

Lacrosse was an important game to many Native Americans in the Southeast. In this painting by George Catlin, some Choctaw men and boys play a game similar to lacrosse. At the time of contact, the Choctaw lived in part of what is now Mississippi. *(Library of Congress, Prints and Photographs Division [LC-USZC4-4810])*

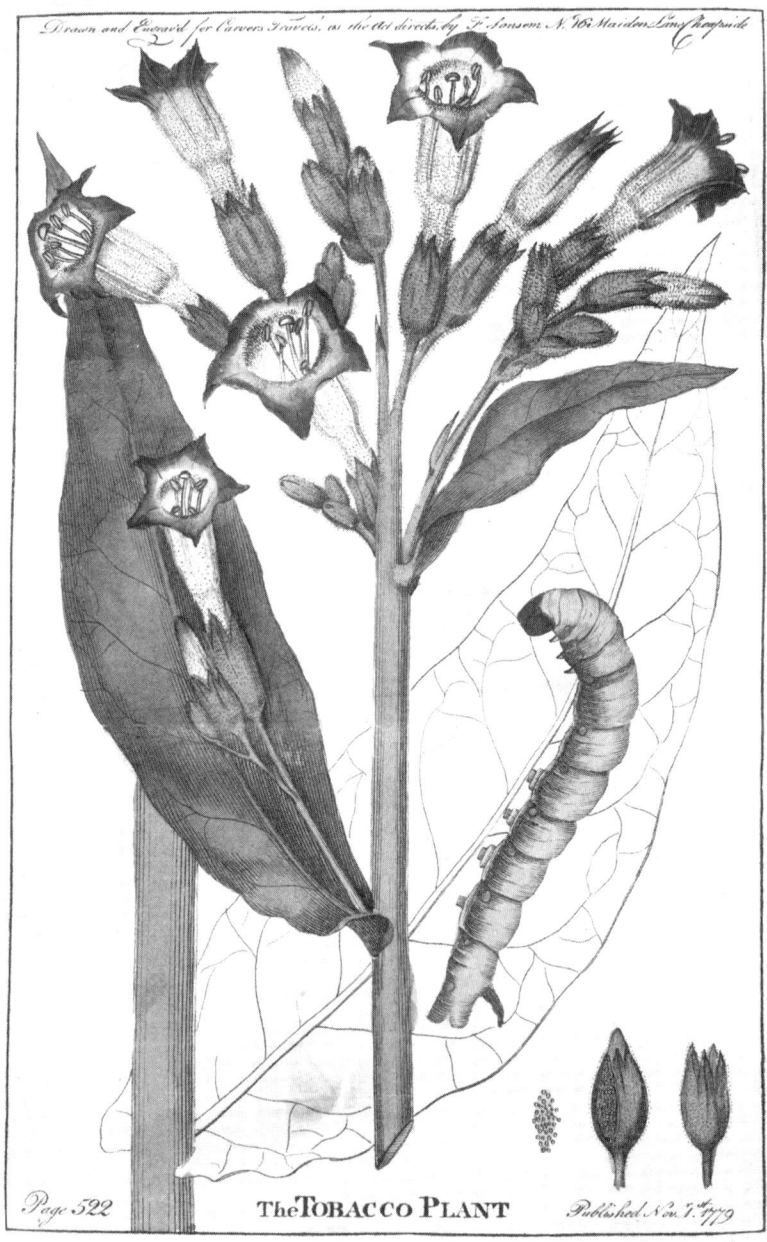

Tobacco, the plant in this 18th-century drawing, was an important crop to many in the Southeast. *(National Archives of Canada)*

of ceremonies and games. The ceremonies were an important part of the life of the village and included events like the Green Corn Festival, which was held each year when the first of the year's corn was ripe enough to be eaten. This was the most important event in the Creek year.

In preparation for the Green Corn Festival, repairs were made to the public buildings and square, and each family cleaned its home and other buildings. The festival served as the beginning of the Creek year. The cooking fires in each family compound were kept going throughout the year as it was not easy to restart a fire. During the festival, all the fires in the village were extinguished and restarted to symbolize the beginning of a new year. At this time, the people in the community were supposed to make a new start as well. They were expected to forget old grudges and forgive their enemies.

Agriculture was the most important activity of the Creek villages. Corn was their most important crop, and like their Mound Builder ancestors, they grew a number of varieties. In addition to corn, they grew squashes, pumpkins, melons, sweet potatoes, and beans. They also grew tobacco, which was smoked in pipes primarily during their ceremonies. In most tribes, the men would help with the heavy work that was needed during the planting

Native Americans used almost every part of the white-tailed deer that they killed. *(National Park Service)*

and harvesting seasons and then the women would do the rest of the work. However, among the Creek, the men worked along with the women in the fields throughout the growing season.

During the harvest season, each family would fill its own granary and then any extra would be stored in communal granaries to provide for the whole tribe in times of shortage. The Creek also supplemented their diets with wild plants and animals. Numerous plants, berries, and nuts were gathered and added to the food of the Creek. The men of the villages also spent a considerable amount of time hunting and fishing. The streams, rivers, lakes, and bays of Georgia teemed with fish and shellfish, and the Indians of the area harvested whatever was available to them. Shellfish were harvested in large quantities. Even some of the early mounds have large piles of shells in their cores.

The forests surrounding the villages also provided numerous animals for the Creek hunters. They hunted with bows and arrows, blowguns, spears, and a variety of traps. Creek hunters were known to hunt for buffalo, bears, wild turkeys, and numerous other small birds and animals. Despite this variety, the most important animal to the Creek, and most of the Indians in the eastern half of North America, was the white-tailed deer.

The white-tailed deer provided meat that was eaten fresh as well as dried to be eaten later. Deerskin was the primary source of material for clothing among the Indians of the Southeast. In addition, most parts of the deer were used in some way. Bones and antlers were made into tools. The deer's hooves were made into rattles. Even the sinew, the tissue surrounding the muscles of an animal, was used like string. When English settlers established their colony in South Carolina, deer hides became an important trade good for the Indians of the Southeast.

The earliest Spanish settlers in Georgia settled along the coast, and their main impact was on the Yamasee. As the Creek traded with the English colonists in South Carolina, they made a number of alliances with the English and often fought with them against other Indian tribes that were allied with the Spanish in Florida and the French in Louisiana. The members of tribes that were defeated by the Creek were often sold to the English traders, who in turn sent them to the sugar plantations of the Caribbean, where they became slaves. This alliance with the English continued throughout the colonial period and through the War of 1812, when the Creek were finally defeated in the Creek War. The leader of the American forces at the time was General Andrew Jackson. Later, in 1830, when Jackson was president, he had most of the rest of the remaining Creek, Cherokee, and other Indians removed from the Southeast and sent to Indian Territory in what is now Oklahoma. Many members of the Creek and other Southeast tribes still live in Oklahoma.

2

The Spanish and French in Georgia

Long before the English established their first permanent colony in North America at Jamestown, Virginia, in 1607, both the French and the Spanish established settlements in what the Spanish called Florida and Carolana: modern-day Florida, North and South Carolina, and Georgia. In 1562, Jean Ribault was granted permission by the admiral of France, Gaspard de Coligny (1519–72), to start a colony in the lands claimed for France by Verrazano in 1524. Coligny and the French had two goals in mind for starting a colony in Carolana. First, they needed a place to send French Protestants, called Huguenots, who were causing problems in Catholic France. Also, the Spanish were shipping large quantities

Huguenots

Like the Puritans in England, the Huguenots in France were Protestants. At first they were tolerated by the Catholic majority. At one point as many as one-quarter of the people in France converted to Protestantism. Many of the nobility and upper classes became Huguenots. Between 1562 and 1598, toleration ended, and there were eight wars between French Huguenots and French Catholics. During this time, many Huguenots left France. Some came to the Americas in search of religious freedom.

Engraved by Theodor de Bry from a painting by Jacques le Moyne, this map shows the French expedition reaching Port Royal Sound in South Carolina. *(Library of Congress, Prints and Photographs Division [LC-USZ62-380])*

of gold, silver, and other valuables from their American colonies back to Spain. The best route to Europe brought the treasure ships along the Carolana coast. A colony there could be used as a base to attack Spanish shipping.

Ribault's first attempt at establishing a colony was a disaster. He and his men came to a large bay, which they named Port Royal Sound, located in modern-day South Carolina. There they built Charlesfort, a small fort where the 26 men Ribault left behind could defend themselves while he returned to France for more settlers.

The men left behind did little work. Rather than plant crops, they traded for food with local Native Americans. When they grew dissatisfied with the man Ribault left in charge, they mutinied. They then built a boat and tried to sail back to France using their

The Spanish and French in Georgia

clothes and bedding for sails. At sea, the men ran out of food and water. It is thought that they resorted to cannibalism before they were rescued by an English ship.

Despite the failure of his first colony, Ribault was determined to create a place for the Huguenots in America. When he returned to France, he found the country embroiled in civil war between the Huguenots and the Catholics. The English were supporting the Huguenot side, and Ribault asked them for help with his attempt to establish a colony. Instead, they put him in prison.

While Ribault was in prison in England, Coligny sponsored another attempt at a colony in 1565. René Goulaine de Laudonnière, who had sailed to America with Ribault on his first voyage,

In 1562, Jean Ribault erected the column in this illustration, portrayed as an object of worship for Native Americans, during his first expedition to Carolana. René Goulaine de Laudonnière (far right) accompanied Ribault on his first expedition and later returned with another group to build Fort Caroline. De Laudonnière is shown here with Timucuan chief Athore. *(Library of Congress, Prints and Photographs Division [LC-USZ62-374])*

Pirates, Privateers, and Spanish Treasure

In the 16th century, Spain ruled the oceans and was the richest and most powerful country in Europe. Much of Spain's wealth came from its colonies in Central and South America. The gold and silver from Spain's American mines and the goods that

(continues)

Born Edward Teach, Blackbeard earned his nickname as a result of his thick, black beard. This image of the pirate originally appeared in an early 18th-century book titled *A General History of Pyrates.* (North Carolina Museum of History)

(continued)

came in to support the Spanish colonies were tempting targets.

Privateers, which were privately owned ships in the employ of a government, were sent out to attack Spanish shipping by both France and England. They attacked cities in the Caribbean and the treasure ships sailing back to Spain. The best route to Europe took the ships up the Gulf Stream past the Carolana coast. It was here that shipping was often attacked. When there was peace in Europe, some privateers kept attacking ships and were then considered pirates. Pirates, who were out to steal fortunes for themselves, used the Carolana coast as a base.

Pedro Menéndez de Avilés helped establish a Spanish fort at St. Augustine in present-day Florida. *(Library of Congress, Prints and Photographs Division [LC-USZ62-102263])*

led a group to the St. Johns River in Florida. There they built Fort Caroline. The small colony was about to suffer the same fate as Charlesfort when Ribault, who had been released from prison in England, arrived with supplies and reinforcements.

At the same time, the Spanish were establishing a fort at St. Augustine in Florida. The leader of the Spanish at St. Augustine, Pedro Menéndez de Avilés had orders to drive the French out of the lands they claimed. Ribault learned of Menéndez's plans and went to sea to attack St. Augustine. Ribault's ships were scattered by a storm, while Menéndez marched up the coast and attacked Fort Caroline. The Spanish took over the fort and killed the French soldiers they captured. Later they found Ribault shipwrecked along the coast and executed him and his remaining men.

In 1566, Menéndez set about building a series of Spanish forts in Carolana. The first Spanish fort along the Georgia coast was on what is today called Saint Catherine's Island. When Menéndez arrived on the island, the local Indian leader was named Guale (pronounced "wallie"). The Spanish used the chief's name to identify the island and eventually applied it to the entire area. The French were not the only ones who hoped to attack the Spanish treasure ships that sailed up the coast before turning east for Europe. Menéndez hoped that forts would prevent pirates and privateers from using the many islands and bays of the Guale region as a base to attack the Spanish treasure ships.

As was the case throughout the Spanish colonies in the Americas, the soldiers were either accompanied by or quickly followed by Catholic priests. Catholic leaders at the Vatican in Rome and Spain believed it was the church's duty to convert as many American Indians as possible to Catholicism. In the 16th century,

Shown in a 1930s photograph by Walker Evans, these ruins are of a Spanish mission located in St. Marys, Georgia. The building is made of tabby, a mixture of lime, sand, and oyster shells. *(Library of Congress, Prints and Photographs Division [LC-USF3301-009057-M3])*

In 1566, Catholic priests established missions on Saint Catherine's and Cumberland Islands, two of the many barrier islands that line the Georgia coast. Cumberland Island is shown here in a contemporary photograph. *(National Park Service)*

Catholic priests set up missions from Florida to California and throughout most of South America. In 1566, the first missions in Georgia were built on what are today called Saint Catherine's and

Cumberland Islands. The Spanish names for the islands were Santa Catalina and San Pedro, respectively.

In addition to converting the Indians to Catholicism, the priests used their converts to supply labor for the missions. Each mission was expected to be self-sufficient, and the recently Christianized Indians did all the work building the mission and working in the mission's fields. The priests also tried to control the Indians in the area of their missions. For the priests in the Guale area this created a serious problem in 1597.

In September 1597, an Indian whom the Spanish called Juanillo was going to become the chief of the Guale-area Indians. Father Pedro Corpa believed that Juanillo had not accepted Christianity and was holding onto what the priest considered pagan ideas. Juanillo did not appreciate the interference of Father Corpa and killed him. Juanillo believed that the priests were just the beginning and that more white people were bound to follow them.

Juanillo and his followers killed four more missionaries and captured a fifth. In a short period of time, most of the Indians in the Guale region had joined in the revolt against the missionaries, When word of the revolt reached Saint Augustine, the governor, Gonzalo Méndez de Canzo, organized a force of 150 soldiers and marched north to the Guale. This large, well-armed force quickly rounded up the Indians who had revolted against the missions. One young Indian who admitted to taking part in the death of one of the priests was executed. Méndez de Canzo intended to sell all the Indians who had been part of the revolt into slavery, but his plan was turned down by officials in Spain.

Juanillo was killed in battle and most of the Indians of the Guale agreed to submit to the authority of Governor Méndez de Canzo. Many of them even traveled to Saint Augustine to meet with him. By 1600, peace had been restored to the Guale area, and the work of the missionaries was resumed. In the early 1600s, there were as many as 38 missions in what would become Georgia and more than 25,000 Indian converts. By this time, the priests had moved inland, and there were missions up

These ruins of a Spanish mission, photographed in 1934, are located in the vicinity of Darien, Georgia, near the Georgia coast. *(Library of Congress, Prints and Photographs Division [HABS, GA,96-DARI.V,1-6])*

the Chattahoochee River as far as modern-day Columbus, Georgia, as well as inland from the original missions along the Atlantic coast.

For more than 100 years, the Spanish had free reign to extend their colonial empire into the southeast corner of North America. However, in 1663, Charles II of England made a land grant for a colony to be called Carolina that included all the land south of Virginia to just south of the Spanish settlement at Saint Augustine, Florida.

CONFLICT BETWEEN THE SPANISH AND THE ENGLISH OVER GEORGIA

In 1670, English colonists arrived in the new colony of Carolina and established their first settlement at what became Charleston, South Carolina, although its settlers originally called it Charles Town. In reaction to the new English settlement, the Spanish at Saint Augustine planned an attack on Charleston, but their ships were hit by a storm when they sailed north. The Spanish abandoned their plan to attack the English but did send more soldiers to their fort on Saint Catherine's Island in 1673.

Charles II ruled England, Scotland, and Ireland from 1660 until his death in 1685. *(Library of Congress, Prints and Photographs Division [LC-USZ62-96910])*

Traders from Carolina were soon involved in profitable trade with the Cherokee, Creek, and Yuchi in Georgia. The English encouraged their Indian trade partners to attack the Spanish missions. Soon many of the inland missions had been attacked, forcing the Spanish to leave the area. During this same time, pirates, who may have had connections in Charleston, attacked the missions on the islands and the coast. By 1686, all the missions in the Guale area had been abandoned.

The missions along the Chattahoochee and the Apalachicola River were also attacked. The Indians who attacked these inland missions were led by Dr. Henry Woodward, an Englishman from

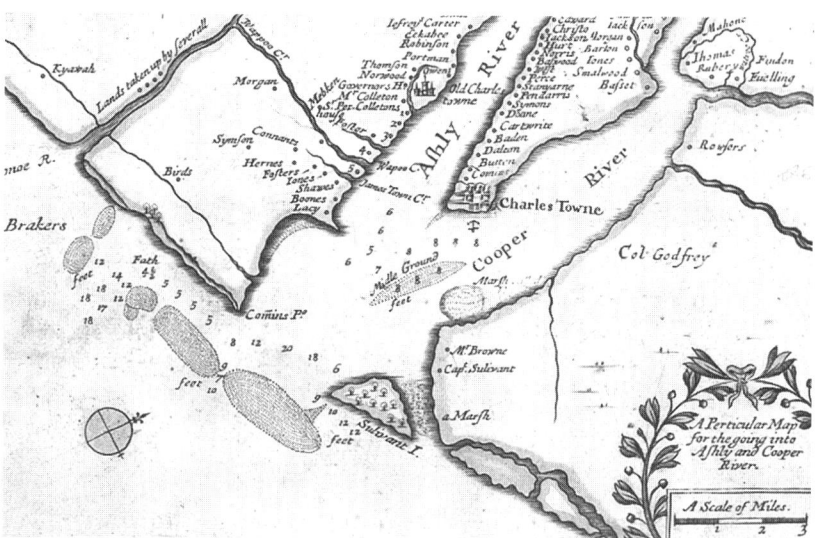

This detail from a 1682 map by Joel Gascoyne shows the area in and around Charles Town, later shortened to Charleston. Originally located on a low, swampy point along the Ashley River, Charleston was moved to more elevated land between the Ashley and Cooper Rivers. *(Library of Congress)*

Dr. Henry Woodward
(ca. 1646–1686)

Dr. Henry Woodward was a surgeon who was probably from Barbados. He moved to North Carolina when he was about 20. In June 1666, he set out with some other people to explore the lands to the south. Woodward was invited to live with a group of Native Americans along the South Carolina coast and became the first Englishman to live in South Carolina. When the Spanish heard about him, they became concerned that he might convince the Native Americans to attack their settlements in Florida. The Spanish went out and captured Woodward.

He was put in prison in St. Augustine but was released by an English privateer who attacked St. Augustine. Woodward then served as a ship's surgeon for a few years. In 1669, he joined a group that was headed to South Carolina to establish a colony. His experience living with the Native Americans along the coast was a valuable asset for the struggling colony as he was able to trade with the Indians for food that helped sustain the colony in its first years.

South Carolina. By 1690, the Spanish had left the area that is now Georgia and retreated below the Saint Mary's River, which is still the boundary between the states of Florida and Georgia.

With the Spanish gone from Georgia, the area was pretty much left to the Creek and other tribes that had allied with the British. However, there continued to be conflicts between the English and Spanish. In 1702, war broke out in Europe between England and the French and Spanish. The part of this war that was fought in North America is known as Queen Anne's War. At the outbreak of war, the South Carolina governor, James Moore, organized an attack on the Spanish at Saint Augustine.

Moore and his force were able to capture the community of Saint Augustine but could not take the solid stone fort that the

Built by the Spanish between 1672 and 1695, Castillo de San Marcos, a large stone fort, protected St. Augustine from attack. *(National Park Service)*

The Margravate of Azilia

In 1717, a Scottish nobleman, Sir Robert Montgomery, approached the English proprietors of the Carolina colonies with a proposal. He wanted to establish a colony of his own in the land between the Savannah and Altamaha Rivers. Sir Robert's plan sounded good to the proprietors for a number of reasons. It meant that the area south of the Savannah River would be settled, and even though Sir Robert would be in charge of the colony as governor for life, control of the land would remain with the proprietors.

Sir Robert envisioned an almost Eden-like colony where numerous exotic crops like silk, olives, and grapes could be grown. He published two pamphlets to generate interest in the colony he called the Margravate of Azilia. The pamphlets were titled *A Discourse Concerning the Design'd Establishment of a New Colony to the South of Carolina, in the Most Delightful Country of the Universe* (1717) and *A Description of the Golden Islands* (1720). Despite the glowing reports of Sir Robert neither he nor the Carolina proprietors were able to raise enough money to start the colony.

Spanish had built there. During this time, there were additional attacks on Spanish missions as well. Although the area that is now Georgia was no longer under the control of the Spanish, the people in South Carolina were still concerned about their security. The Spanish still held Florida, and the French had established control in Louisiana. The main concern for the people in South Carolina was not expanding their colony but losing their trading territory. By this time, their trading network extended west to the Mississippi River.

Some in South Carolina proposed a number of schemes to establish English settlements on the Mississippi and the land in between. None of these early proposals were acted upon because in 1715 the Yamassee tribes of South Carolina went to war and almost succeeded in wiping out the colony of South Carolina. After finally defeating the Yamassee in 1716, the colonists in South Carolina renewed their interests in expanding European settlement south of the Savannah River.

During the first quarter of the 18th century, there were a number of proposals for settlement in what would become Georgia,

The French Huguenots from Switzerland that Purry sent up the Savannah River decided to settle in swampy land bordering the river than on a bluff. The town they founded, Purrysburgh, was likely located on land similar to that in this photograph of the Savannah River near Savannah, Georgia. *(National Archives, Still Picture Records [NWDNS-165-SC-47])*

but none seemed to work out. Sir Robert Montgomery's proposal for a personal colony never got off the ground because of lack of money. A proposal from Jean-Pierre Purry of Switzerland was intended for land south of the Savannah River. Although Purrysburgh came into existence, it ended up on the South Carolina side of the Savannah River.

Purry believed that the perfect climate for people and agriculture existed at 33° latitude. Purry had suggested to the Dutch that he be allowed to establish a colony in either their colony in South Africa or Australia and was turned down. When he brought his proposal to the English, they agreed to let him try his experiment along the Savannah River. However, Purry picked a low, swampy area along the north bank of the river and established his community in South Carolina. The Swiss people he settled there suffered greatly. By 1800, Purrysburgh had disappeared.

It must have seemed to many that the lands of Georgia, with the exception of a couple of trading posts, would remain empty of European settlement. Ideas continued to be suggested in both South Carolina and England, but circumstances continued to prevent expansion of the colony across the Savannah River. However, social problems in England and a member of the British Parliament named James Edward Oglethorpe combined to finally establish the English colony of Georgia.

The English Colony of Georgia

James Edward Oglethorpe was a member of the English upper class and became a member of Parliament in 1722. During his first six years in Parliament, Oglethorpe did little to distinguish

A visit to his friend Robert Castell in Fleet Prison in London (where he died) inspired Oglethorpe to work for changes in prison conditions. The prison is shown in an 1809 illustration. *(The Bridgeman Art Library)*

himself. Then, in 1728, a close friend of his, architect Robert Castell, was sent to prison because he could not pay his debts. Castell was sent to the Fleet Prison in London, where conditions were terrible for the prisoners. To make matters worse, Castell was unable to come up with any money to pay the warden for preferential treatment. Therefore, he was put in the worst part of the prison where many of the inmates were suffering from smallpox.

Castell became sick with smallpox and soon died. Oglethorpe had visited his friend in prison and considered the conditions there responsible for Castell's death. Oglethorpe took it upon himself to do something about the dreadful conditions in England's prisons. In February 1729, he was appointed chairman of a committee in Parliament to investigate the country's prisons. As a result of the committee's work, a few of the worst wardens were prosecuted for their mistreatment of prisoners. In addition, approximately 10,000 prisoners were released.

Often referred to as the founder of Georgia, General James Edward Oglethorpe was primarily concerned with the colony's defense, especially protecting the colony from the Spanish in Florida. *(Courtesy of Hargrett Rare Book & Manuscript Library/University of Georgia Libraries)*

Most of the prisoners who Oglethorpe got released were debtors. At the time, people who could not pay their debts were put in prison. This created a bad situation because the only way they could get out of prison was to pay their debts, and there was no way for them to earn money while in prison. Oglethorpe became well-known for his investigation of the prisons, and many religious and philanthropic leaders praised him.

The release of all those debtors from prison made many in England wonder what should be done with them. Oglethorpe had come to know one of the leading philanthropists of the time, Dr. Thomas Bray. It seems likely that Dr. Bray originally had the idea of creating a colony for England's poor in America. However, when he died in 1730, it fell to Oglethorpe to make the idea a reality. Later in 1730, Oglethorpe led a number of Dr. Bray's followers in applying to King George II's government for a charter to create a colony in America.

Most of the knowledgeable people in England were aware of the ongoing need for additional settlement in America between the Spanish in Florida and the English colony of South Carolina. It was there that Oglethorpe suggested his group be granted a colony to be named Georgia after the king. George II and his advisers thought the colony of Georgia was a good idea, and the charter for the colony was passed by the Privy Council on January 27, 1732. The king signed it in the spring of that year, and the charter was officially granted on June 9, 1732.

The charter was unique among the many charters that had been granted over the years of English colonization in North America. First, it created a board of trustees to oversee the colony. Unlike proprietors in other colonies, the trustees were prohibited by the charter from profiting in the colony. They were given political control, but it was to last for only 21 years. During that time, the governor and primary officials were subject to Crown approval. What was lacking in the charter was a provision for any type of legislative assembly in the colony. The power to make rules and laws for the colony rested with the trustees.

Oglethorpe and the other trustees held high hopes and ideals for Georgia. They thought that the climate was perfect for mulberry trees for silkworms, olive trees, grape vines, and other valuable crops that could not be grown in England's cool, damp climate. They also hoped to make Georgia a model colony whose people would be happy and productive. The fact that religious toleration

George II, king of Great Britain and Ireland from 1727 until 1760, granted Oglethorpe the charter for the colony of Georgia in 1732. *(Library of Congress, Prints and Photographs Division [LC-USZ62-64702])*

James Edward Oglethorpe
(ca. 1696–1785)

James Edward Oglethorpe was born in London on December 22, 1696. His father, Theophilus Oglethorpe, was a colonel in the British army and a member of the English upper class. James Oglethorpe was brought up among the privileged and attended Eton and Oxford University. At the age of 14, he followed in the family's tradition and joined the army, where he rose to the rank of captain in the elite Queen's Guard. When he was 20, Oglethorpe resigned from the British army and went to the European Continent. He joined the army of Prince Eugene of Savoy, in what is today Austria, and distinguished himself in fighting against the Turks. He also spent time at the French court before returning to England in 1719.

He was first elected to Parliament in 1722 and held his seat until 1743. During this time, he gained a widespread following in England for his work in reforming the country's prisons. As a result of these efforts, he became involved in the attempt to establish a colony in America for former debtors. Although a number of the early colonists were drawn from the poor of England, very few were actually debtors.

Oglethorpe's ideas were an integral part of the ideas behind the founding of the colony of Georgia. Although he made two trips back to England during the early years of the colony, he remained the leader of Georgia from 1733 to 1743, when he returned to England for good. He lived to be 88 years old, and when he died in 1785, he was well-known through Great Britain.

for all Christians except Catholics was written into the charter indicates the type of colony the trustees wanted.

As soon as the trustees received the charter for Georgia, they began recruiting potential colonists. Despite Oglethorpe's concerns for the plight of England's debtors, the people who were recruited to settle in Georgia were not necessarily debtors. The idea that Georgia was a debtors' colony is one of those stories that has been told so many times that people believed it was true. The people the trustees selected to send to Georgia were drawn from what was referred to as the "unfortunate poor"; they were known as "charity colonists." Most of the heads of the families that were sent to Georgia by the trustees were tradesmen and artisans who were either out of work or struggling to get by.

Silk

Both the Swiss colonist Jean-Pierre Purry, who had settled in South Carolina, and the Georgia trustees hoped to plant mulberry trees and introduce silkworms in North America. Although neither group succeeded in creating an American silk industry, their desire to do so shows they understood the need for a cash crop for the colony. South Carolinian colonists had become rich growing rice and indigo—a plant that can be used to make a blue dye. Further north in North Carolina, Virginia, and Maryland, great fortunes had been created growing tobacco. Because of Georgia's latitude, it was believed that mulberry trees and the silkworms that feed on them would succeed there. It is in the cocoons of the silkworms that the fiber for silk thread is found. If this had worked, Georgia might have eclipsed the other colonies in creating wealth for its planters.

Silk originated in China, where its manufacture was kept secret for thousands of years. For the Chinese, silk was one of their most valuable exports. Around A.D. 550 two Roman monks were sent to China and successfully smuggled out mulberry tree seeds and silkworm eggs in their hollowed out walking sticks. Because of this, silk manufacture spread to the West and was successfully established around the Mediterranean Sea. However, attempts to establish mulberry trees in England were a complete failure, and the English had to continue to import silk, which remained very expensive. The idea of England creating its own source of silk was one of the hopes for the Georgia colony.

The list of early colonists shows professions such as smith, carpenter, tanner, bookbinder, servant, and other members of England's lower class. In advertising and interviewing for prospective charity colonists, the trustees promised that they would be supported for one year and receive 50 acres of land for their family. Another type of colonist that was accepted to go to Georgia was known as an "adventurer." Adventurers paid for their passage to Georgia and were promised 500 acres in the colony. Hundreds of people applied to go to Georgia, and 114 people representing about 35 families were selected to be among the first residents of Georgia.

Included in this group were Oglethorpe, who was the only trustee to ever see Georgia; Dr. William Cox, who had volunteered to provide medical aid to the colony; and the Reverend Henry

This 1732 map was the first to show the colony of Georgia. Also visible on this map are Florida and South Carolina. *(Courtesy of Hargrett Rare Book & Manuscript Library/University of Georgia Libraries)*

Herbert, who had volunteered to be the colony's minister. The trustees hired the ship *Ann* to transport the colonists, their supplies and livestock to Georgia. The *Ann* set sail on November 17, 1732, sailing down the Thames from Gravesend and then heading east to America.

OGLETHORPE AND THE COLONISTS ARRIVE IN GEORGIA

For many colonists who traveled to North America in the 17th century, the trip across the North Atlantic was extremely hard. By 1732, when the colonists headed for Georgia, ships had become larger and better outfitted to prevent disease and malnutrition. On the *Ann*, the colonists were fed a decent and varied diet and, when possible, spent time on deck in the fresh ocean air. During the crossing, two infants died. However, Oglethorpe reported that they were both ill when they had come aboard in England. There was one birth while the colonists were at sea. The little boy was named Georgius Marinus Warren. *Georgius* was in honor of their destination, and *Marinus* indicated that he was born on a ship. Dr. Cox assisted in his delivery, and Reverend Henry Herbert christened him with Oglethorpe standing as the boy's godfather. It was during the crossing of the Atlantic that the colonists began calling Oglethorpe father and looking to him for leadership although he had no official position.

On January 13, 1733, the *Ann* arrived off the coast of Charles Town, South Carolina. Governor Robert Johnson of South Carolina suggested that the colonists be kept on their ship. It is thought that he feared if they came ashore in Charles Town they would want to stay there and not go on to Georgia. The governor and other South Carolinians wanted to make sure that this time a colony to their south came into being. Oglethorpe did go ashore and presented a copy of the Georgia charter to Johnson. To show their support for the new colony, the South Carolina assembly voted to help their new neighbors.

A large number of cattle and pigs and a substantial quantity of rice were promised to Oglethorpe for his colony. In addition, the assembly offered to help the colonists get to the site of their first town and provide scouts and rangers to help them pick a spot. Some have speculated that the South Carolinians already had a spot in mind for Georgia's first settlement. It is unlikely that Oglethorpe would have found as ideal a location without help.

Oglethorpe left the colonists at Port Royal and Beaufort, South Carolina, and went off to find a spot for his colony. He returned on January 24 to tell the colonists he had found the perfect location. The place he had chosen, with the help of his South Carolina guides, was known as Yamacraw Bluff, and it was about 17 miles up the Savannah River. The bluff stood about 40 feet above the river and was flat on top. There were good stands of pine in the area

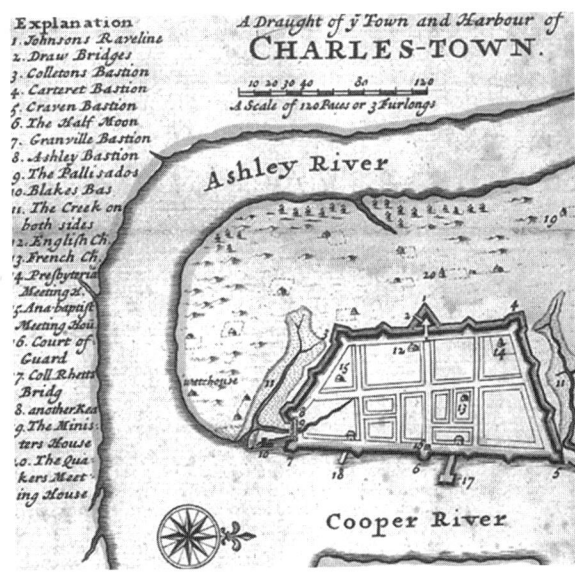

When Oglethorpe and his colonists arrived in 1733, colonists at Charles Town helped them find a location for their first town. This detail of a 1715 map by Herman Moll focuses on Charles Town's main settlement, especially the harbor, between the Ashley and Cooper Rivers. The complicated figure on the Cooper River side of the settlement represents the large fort the town contained. *(Library of Congress)*

that could supply wood for building houses for the colonists. The only Indians in the area were a small village of about 100 Creek who referred to themselves as the Yamacraw. These Indians had broken away from a much larger group of Creek who lived several hundred miles to the west.

The leader of the Yamacraw was named Tomochichi, and he welcomed Oglethorpe and the colonists to the area. There was also a trading post on Yamacraw Bluff that was run by John Musgrove and his wife Mary, who was half English and half Creek. Mary served as a translator for Oglethorpe in his dealings with Tomochichi and the other Indians. It was Oglethorpe and the trustees' plan to deal fairly with the Indians who already lived in Georgia. In May 1733, Oglethorpe arranged a meeting between himself and 50 *miccos* from the lower Creek. He presented each of the chiefs with presents and negotiated a peace treaty with the Creek.

Oglethorpe and the colonists he led negotiated with the Creek Indians (who referred to themselves as the Yamacraw) for the land that would eventually become known as Savannah. *(Courtesy of Hargrett Rare Book & Manuscript Library/University of Georgia Libraries)*

Tomochichi (left) was leader of the Yamacraw and negotiated with the English colonists on behalf of his tribe. The boy on the right is his nephew Toonahowi. *(Courtesy of Hargrett Rare Book & Manuscript Library/University of Georgia Libraries)*

LAYING OUT SAVANNAH

Oglethorpe chose to name his new settlement after the river on which it was located, and he and the colonists arrived at the future site of Savannah, Georgia, on February 12, 1733. This date is still considered the birth date of Georgia. By the time

Oglethorpe sailed for Georgia, there had been advances made in the ideas of how a town and a city should be designed. Oglethorpe, with the aid of Colonel William Bull, an engineer from South Carolina, put these ideas to work in the layout of Savannah.

Each family received a lot in town, five acres for vegetable gardens near town, and 45 acres for farming farther out. The adventurers' farms were much bigger, as they had been promised a total of 500 acres. Although slavery was not originally allowed in Georgia, black sawyers from South Carolina were sent by Governor Johnson to help turn the tall pines of Yamacraw Bluff into lumber to build the houses for the colonists. At first, everyone lived in tents, but the building of houses progressed rapidly as did the town's defenses.

A palisade was constructed around the town, and two blockhouses were built to defend it. Cannons were placed in the block-

City Planning

The cities of Europe had grown haphazardly over hundreds of years and were often crowded and dirty. After a fire burned a large section of London in 1666, Sir Christopher Wren, who became a famous architect, came up with a plan for redesigning the destroyed part of London. His plan called for straight, wide streets and numerous open parks. Property disputes prevented his plan from being put into effect, but the ideas he put forth were adopted by many.

Philadelphia, Pennsylvania, had been laid out using the modern (at the time) ideas of city planning, and Bull and Oglethorpe put those ideas to work in Savannah. Straight streets divided the flat land on Yamacraw Bluff into identical blocks. The blocks were divided into five lots on each side, with an alley splitting the block. Each of the 10 lots was to have an identical single-story, wooden house that was 16 feet wide and 24 feet long. Every four blocks were considered a ward and had a public square at its center. The squares were 270 by 315 feet, and the lots around the square were reserved for shops, churches, and other public buildings. The original layout consisted of six wards. The plan worked so well that Savannah continued to follow it as it grew over the next 100 years. The plan was also followed by the towns in Georgia that were established after Savannah.

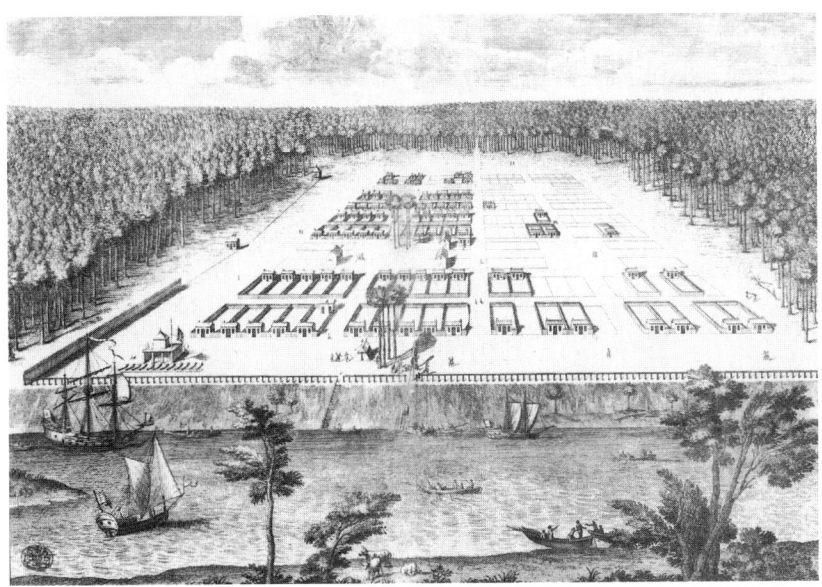

Colonel William Bull and James Edward Oglethorpe designed Savannah so that it had straight, wide streets and blocks of land with public squares arranged throughout, as shown in this image of the city in 1734. *(Library of Congress)*

houses, and six cannons were set up along the bluff in case the Spanish ever decided to attack Savannah. Although the trustees had not sent any soldiers to help defend Georgia, Oglethorpe had begun training and drilling the male colonists even before they left England. Oglethorpe claimed that he could put a force of 70 colonists in the field if needed, and he continued to drill them in Savannah. He often held shooting competitions that offered prizes to help people become better shots.

The biggest problem during the first year in Georgia was the number of colonists who died during the first summer. In the northern colonies, it had always been the long winters that took a heavy toll on the first settlers. In Georgia, it was the summers. Oglethorpe believed that the colonists' fondness for rum was the major problem, but it was much more complicated than that. Although Savannah was built on high ground, there were numerous swamps in the area that were breeding grounds for hordes of mosquitoes and other biting insects. Mosquitoes especially were known to transmit a number of diseases. In addition,

The swamps of the Okefenokee National Wildlife Refuge in southeastern Georgia, shown in a contemporary photograph, are typical of the swampy areas near Savannah that served as breeding grounds for insects that spread disease among early colonists in Georgia. *(U.S. Fish & Wildlife Service)*

The Diseases Faced by the Colonists in Georgia

The healthy climate of North America presented very few threats to the colonists. They also had a certain amount of immunity to the diseases they brought with them that wiped out so many Native Americans. However, two diseases brought to South Carolina from Africa by slaves threatened the colonists in Georgia.

Yellow fever and malaria are both blood-borne diseases that are transmitted from one human to another by mosquitoes. Yellow fever is a virus that attacks the blood and the liver. As the liver becomes overloaded from the disease, it cannot process the bile that it usually eliminates, and the afflicted person turns yellow. There is still no known treatment for yellow fever, and it often kills people within four to eight days. Today, a vaccine exists to prevent it. In colonial times, those who survived yellow fever became immune, and it never reoccurred in them.

Malaria is actually a single-cell parasite that feeds on the red blood cells in the body. The parasites are born in the host mosquitoes that then transmit them to humans. The disease causes high fever combined with shaking and chills. In severe cases it is fatal. Approximately 300 to 500 million people a year still contract malaria. As many as 2.5 million people still die each year from the disease. Controlling mosquitoes in North America has eliminated the disease in the United States.

the colonists depended on the river and other surface water for drinking. Often this water was contaminated and caused dysentery and other physical problems. During the first summer, approximately 40 people died of disease. One of the first was Dr. Cox.

The situation looked bleak for Savannah without its doctor. However, on July 11, 1733, an unexpected group of colonists arrived in Savannah. This group consisted of a number of Jews who hoped that the promised religious freedom of Georgia would apply to them as well. Among the Jews was Dr. Samuel Nunis. Dr. Nunis immediately began administering to the sick of Savannah, and many of his patients fully recovered. When officials in London learned that Oglethorpe had allowed Jews to settle in Georgia, they ordered him to expel them. Oglethorpe refused and ever since Savannah has had a large and welcomed Jewish community.

In this 1733 map, the area of the British empire in North America is clearly visible. *(Courtesy of Hargrett Rare Book & Manuscript Library/University of Georgia Libraries)*

In addition to the Jews, settlers came from other colonies, England, and other European countries to be a part of Georgia. The colony still faced numerous problems. However, the experiences of more than 100 years of English colonization in North

America and the strong leadership of Oglethorpe made the founding of Georgia much less of an ordeal than what many of the other 12 colonies had faced.

4

Life in Colonial Georgia

During the early years of Georgia, growth was very slow. By 1740, just over 2,000 settlers lived in the colony. Most if not all of the colonists were of European descent. Ten years later, in

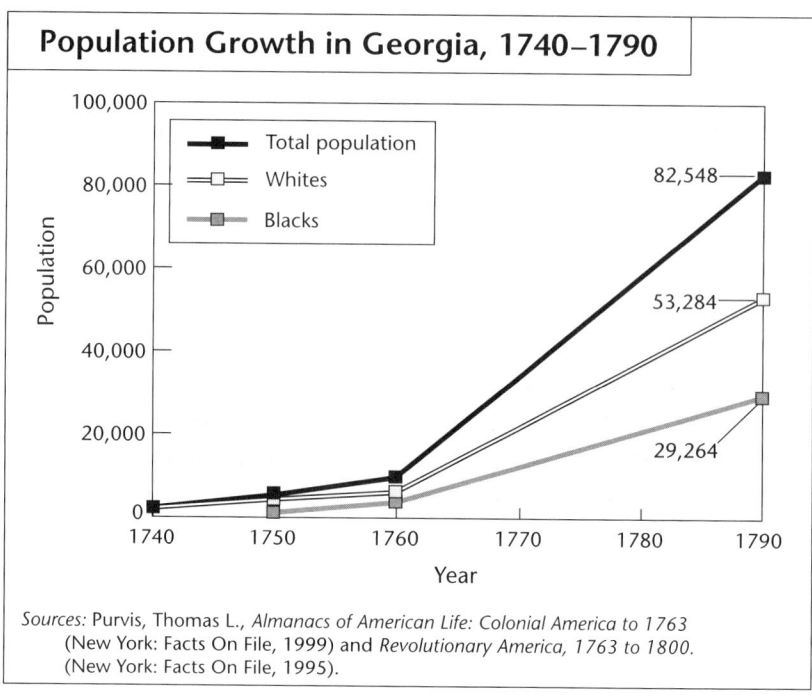

Georgia was the last of the 13 colonies to be established and grew slowly until after the American Revolution.

1750, there were just over 5,000 people in the colony, and about 20 percent of them were of African descent. By 1760, the population had reached almost 10,000 people, but Georgia remained the least-populated of the thirteen colonies. By comparison, Delaware, which had the next fewest number of residents, boasted more than 33,000 people. At the time, Virginia was the largest colony, with almost 340,000 people.

There were many reasons for the slow growth of Georgia. The land restrictions of 50 acres for charity colonists and 500 for adventurers prevented the type of plantation economy that had developed in other parts of the South. There were also rules in Georgia with which many people did not want to comply. Oglethorpe was opposed to excessive drinking and to slavery. He convinced the trustees that rum and slaves had no place in Georgia. Oglethorpe also controlled the settlement of Georgia. He tried to force people into small and often remote communities that were intended to aid in the defense of the colony. These communities consisted of 10 families who built their homes around a small, strategically located fort.

EARLY SETTLERS AND SETTLEMENTS IN GEORGIA

Many who had come to the American colonies had left Europe because of religious persecution. At the time, Protestants and Catholics remained intolerant of each other. In England, at one time or another anyone who was not a member of the official Church of England was persecuted. The Puritans of New England and the Quakers of Pennsylvania set up their colonies so they could practice their versions of Protestantism without interference. Maryland was originally intended as a haven for English Catholics. Other religious groups came to the colonies seeking a place to worship as they saw fit.

In Georgia at least three, who would become well known religious leaders, came with the intent of converting Indians to Christianity. John Wesley, Charles Wesley, and George Whitefield came to Georgia in the early years of the colony and their experiences there influenced their thinking. John Wesley arrived in Georgia in 1735 on a ship that carried a number of Moravians. He credited the simple beliefs of these German protestants with having an impact on his own religious thinking. John Wesley spent three years in Georgia. Charles Wesley accompanied his brother to Georgia and spent a year as Oglethorpe's secretary before he was forced to return to England for health reasons. Whitefield followed the Wesleys to Georgia but also stayed only a short period of time. On a second trip to the colonies Whitefield became involved in a religious movement in New England known as the Great Awakening.

John Wesley and his brother Charles visited colonial Georgia as missionaries in 1735. John later experienced a religious conversion and went on to found the Protestant denomination of Methodism. *(Library of Congress, Prints and Photographs Division [LC-USZ62-5824])*

Charles Wesley accompanied his brother John as a missionary to colonial Georgia and later helped him establish Methodism. *(Library of Congress, Prints and Photographs Division [LC-USZ6-546])*

One such group came to Georgia in its second year. At the time, the German-speaking people of the Salzburg region, which is in modern-day Austria, were subjects of the Holy Roman Empire and ruled by the archbishop of Salzburg. Many of the people in the area had become Protestants and were members of the Lutheran Church. By the early 1730s, the archbishop had forced approximately 30,000 Salzburg Protestants to leave the area. As the most powerful Protestant country in the world, England took an interest in the persecution of the Salzburgers. A group known as the Society for Promoting Christian Knowledge

Life in Colonial Georgia

The Methodist Church

When John Wesley, Charles Wesley, and George Whitefield were students at Oxford University in England in 1729, they belonged to a group of students who gathered together to worship. The other students called them the "Holy Club" or the "Methodists" because of the methodical way they went about practicing religion. After their experiences in Georgia, the three began preaching sermons outdoors as they were not welcome in any churches in England. As the number of their followers grew, they formed into the religious movement that created the Methodist Church.

Eventually John Wesley and Whitefield disagreed over matters of theology and Whitefield formed his own church known as Calvinistic Methodists. Charles Wesley spent much of the rest of his life writing religious music for the new church that his brother founded. Charles is credited with writing over 7,000 Methodist hymns.

George Whitefield, a minister native to Great Britain, made several trips to the British colonies in North America to preach to the colonists. *(Library of Congress, Prints and Photographs Division [LC-USZ62-120395])*

suggested to the Georgia trustees that the Salzburgers would be good for Georgia.

At first, the trustees did not have enough money to pay for the Salzburgers to move to Georgia. However, Parliament granted the trustees £10,000 to help with the cost of sending charity colonists to Georgia. With part of this money, the trustees agreed to send a group of Salzburgers to Georgia. In 1734, 42 families of Salzburgers sailed to Georgia. Oglethorpe selected a site for them on a tributary of the Savannah River about 22 miles from Savannah. The site seemed ideal at first. The Salzburgers called their community Ebenezer and immediately went to work clearing the land and building their town. However, by the end of 1734, the Salzburgers were discouraged.

The soil at Ebenezer was rather poor and the low-lying location was causing a number of health problems for the people. At the time, Oglethorpe was on a trip to England and the Salzburgers had to make the best of it until he returned. When Oglethorpe returned, a new location for the Salzburgers, six miles away on Red Bluff next to the Savannah River, was chosen as the second site for

In 1734, a group of Salzburger families, German-speaking people from the Salzburg region, sailed to colonial Georgia. Their first settlement was called Ebenezer. *(North Wind Picture Archives)*

their community. The community was called New Ebenezer, and a large number of other Salzburgers joined their countrypeople there, becoming Georgians.

In addition to the Salzburgers, other early settlements were established by groups of people from Scotland. One group of Scots founded the community of Darien, which is located at the mouth of the Altamaha River. Another group of Scots settled at Joseph's Town on the Savannah River and at Sterling Bluff on the Ogeechee River. Neither of these communities succeeded, and the people who survived moved to Savannah. The Scots in Savannah organized themselves into a group called the Saint Andrews Club and came to oppose many of Oglethorpe's plans.

Another group of German-speaking Protestants who arrived in Georgia were members of the Moravian church. Most of these people arrived as indentured servants and ended up in Savannah.

Indentured Servants

The original leaders of the efforts to colonize North America intended to use the structured society of England as their model. They foresaw a landed nobility served by a working class. The question was how to get people willing to be laborers and servants to agree to go the colonies. Starting with Virginia and continuing throughout the colonial period, a system of forced workers known as indentured servants was used in all the colonies.

Many of the original colonists in the English colonies arrived as indentured servants. These people signed an agreement to work for a term of four to seven years. In exchange for their labor, they received transportation to the colony; food, clothing, and shelter; and free land at the end of their indenture. Some have estimated that during the 17th and 18th centuries between one-half and two-thirds of all people who came to the English colonies in North America arrived as indentured servants.

The terms of indenture were transferable. Often ship captains held the indenture papers and would sell them upon arrival in the colonies. In the 17th century, as plantations in the South grew in size and wealth, it was through the labor of indentured servants. As time went on, the planters of Virginia, Maryland, the Carolinas, and eventually Georgia found a cheaper source of labor, and indentured servants were replaced by slaves from Africa.

Later, when Georgia was forced to fight the Spanish, the pacifist beliefs of the Moravians caused them to be at odds with the rest of the colonists in Georgia.

During these early years, the trustees continued to interview and select charity colonists. During the first six years of the colony, a total of approximately 1,400 charity colonists were sent to Georgia. For the most part, the ideas championed by the trustees failed. The colonists they chose to send were often ill-prepared for life in Georgia. Tradesmen and artisans from the cities of England did not have the skills needed to thrive in a frontier environment like Georgia. Many of the defensive communities that Oglethorpe set up never had their full number of 10 families. A number of them were soon abandoned because, despite their strategic locations, they were not very good spots for farming. The trustees found that often the year of promised food was not enough, and the cost of maintaining those already in the colony limited their ability to recruit new colonists. After 1738, the practice of sponsoring charity colonists was all but abandoned.

A few of Oglethorpe's defensive communities did survive. Frederica on Saint Simons Island was founded to help defend the coast from the Spanish in Florida. Saint Simons Island was such a pleasant place that Oglethorpe had a cottage built there, which probably made him the first Georgian to have a second house at the beach. Other defensive communities were established upriver at Augusta and at Thunderbolt, south of Savannah on the Wilmington River.

Farming was the major activity in Georgia. However, the exotic crops envisioned by Oglethorpe and the trustees never made it in the colony. The summer heat and a lack of available laborers made it hard for those trying to farm. Some Georgians practiced a number of deceptions to bring slaves from South Carolina to Georgia.

SLAVERY IN GEORGIA

As deplorable as slavery was, it was allowed in all of the English colonies except Georgia. In 1740, South Carolina, the colony closest to Georgia, had twice as many slaves as people of European descent. The plantations of South Carolina produced large quantities of rice and indigo for export. The plantation owners of South

Although Georgia did not legally permit slavery before 1750, many landowners found ways around that restriction. In this 1850s illustration, slaves pick cotton on a Georgia plantation. *(Library of Congress, Prints and Photographs Division [LC-USZ62-76385])*

Carolina were some of the wealthiest people in the colonies. At first there were no slaves allowed in Georgia, but people soon thought of ways to get around the laws.

Some landowners in Georgia also had plantations in South Carolina and just brought some of their slaves to work their Georgia farms. Others figured out a way to rent slaves. These landowners would make a deal with a plantation owner in South Carolina to "rent" slaves and bring them to Georgia. Although these people technically did not own the slaves, the fact that some of the rental contracts were for 100 years made it apparent that they had no intention of ever sending their rented slaves back to South Carolina.

When Oglethorpe left Georgia in 1743, the trustees lifted the ban on rum. They also changed the rules and allowed people

Slavery

Slavery has existed in many civilizations throughout history. Slaves built the Great Wall of China and the pyramids in Egypt. The Roman Empire might not have existed without the labor of untold numbers of slaves. The American colonies, especially those from Maryland south, would probably not have prospered without slave labor.

The slaves that came to the Americas traveled what was called the middle passage from Africa to the Americas. The passage would take between 25 and 60 days, depending on wind conditions. During that time, the future slaves were poorly treated, getting a small allotment of food twice a day. The slaves were brought up on deck during the day, but the men were kept in shackles. The women and children were often allowed to move about freely. At night or if the weather was bad, the slaves were forced to remain below deck where they were allowed only as much space as was needed to lie down.

During this middle passage, a number of the slaves often died. The percentage who died depended on the weather: The

(continues)

Slavery became legal in Georgia in 1750. Constructed in 1758, this pavilion in the public square of present-day Louisville, Georgia, was originally used as a market to sell slaves. *(Library of Congress, Prints and Photographs Division [HABS, GA,82-LOUVI,1-1])*

(continued)

longer the trip and/or the more they were confined below deck, the more died. Spoiled food or contaminated water also killed many on the slave ships. The development of faster ships in the second half of the 18th century and a better understanding of diseases like dysentery and scurvy cut down on the number who died in the middle passage.

It is estimated that more than 10 million Africans traveled the middle passage into slavery in the Americas. Many of those who came died within a few years. In the first official census of the United States in 1790, there were almost 700,000 slaves in a total population of just over 3.9 million people.

Slaves made up a large percentage of Georgia's population after the colony legalized slavery in 1750. These cabins served as housing for slaves on a plantation in the vicinity of Columbus, Georgia. *(Library of Congress, Prints and Photographs Division [HABS, GA,108-COLM.V, 2-1])*

to own thousand of acres in Georgia. Seven years later, in 1750, they changed their policy on slavery. By the end of the year, there were approximately 1,000 blacks in the colony, and almost all of them were slaves. Ten years later, in 1760, there were more than 3,500 blacks in Georgia, and they made up over one-third of the population of the colony. When the first official United States census was taken in 1790, Georgia's population had grown to 82,548 people and 29,264 of them were slaves. Without the relatively cheap labor provided by slaves and the rice plantations that they worked, Georgia might have continued to struggle economically.

THE WAR OF JENKINS' EAR

Between 1689 and 1762, France and Great Britain fought four wars. Although the major parts of these wars took place in Europe, the wars spilled over into French and English colonies around the world. The North American battles of the four wars are called the French and Indian wars. The other superpower at the time was Spain. Spain was often involved in the French and Indian wars as an ally of France. Prior to the third war, known in North America as King George's War (1744–48), Spain and Great Britain were at war from 1739 to 1744.

This war between Spain and Great Britain was known as the War of Jenkins' Ear and was fought for two main reasons. Probably most important was the desire of British merchants to be allowed to trade with Spanish colonies in the Americas and elsewhere. In the early 1730s, British merchants who traded with a Spanish

Life in Colonial Georgia

This 1741 map of the Georgia coast includes such interesting details as a label for the location of the Yamacraw Indians and Savannah's grid design at the mouth of the Savannah River. Drawn in detail in an inset in the bottom right corner is St. Simon's Island, including Fort Frederica, which Oglethorpe built in 1736. *(Courtesy of Hargrett Rare Book & Manuscript Library/University of Georgia Libraries)*

colony were breaking the law, and their ships were seized by the Spanish if they were caught. The other part of the disagreement between the two countries involved Georgia.

The years leading up to the war had been a tense time for the struggling colony of Georgia. The Spanish made it known that they believed Florida included all the land up to Port Royal, South Carolina. At the same time, the English claimed that their territory went to latitude 29° south, which was below Saint Augustine. In 1736, the English sent Captain Charles Dempsey to Georgia to try and prevent fighting with the Spanish in Florida. Dempsey was able to negotiate a treaty in a meeting held at Frederica on Saint Simons Island with Governor Francisco de Moral Sanchez of Florida. But when the treaty arrived at the Spanish capital of Madrid, the government rejected it and recalled Sanchez from Saint Augustine.

Oglethorpe was truly concerned about the security of his colony. On November 23, 1736, he left Georgia for London in hopes of convincing Parliament and the Crown to provide adequate protection for Georgia. After much negotiating, Parliament voted £20,000 for the defense of the colony. The government in London also supplied Oglethorpe with a regiment of 700 troops to go back to America with him. When he got back to Georgia in September 1738, Oglethorpe stationed his regiment at Fort Saint Simon and began trying to strengthen the colony's defenses.

On October 3, 1739, Oglethorpe and the other leaders in Savannah declared war on Florida based on a false report from a Rhode Island merchant ship captain that war had started in Europe. The official start of the war for the Crown actually came two weeks later and did not arrive in Georgia until the following spring. In

Jenkins' Ear

In 1731, a British merchant ship was caught trying to smuggle goods into Florida. When the Spanish coast guard captured the ship's captain, Robert Jenkins, he claimed they cut off his ear. Seven years later, in 1738, as Parliament was debating the idea of declaring war on Spain, Captain Jenkins stood up in Parliament and held up what he claimed was the shriveled remains of his ear. Jenkins's gruesome display and explanation of the loss of his ear at the hands of the Spanish influenced Parliament to vote for the war that continues to be called the War of Jenkins' Ear.

Life in Colonial Georgia

Oglethorpe led an unsuccessful expedition to attack Castillo de San Marcos, the fort at St. Augustine, in 1740. *(North Wind Picture Archives)*

1740, Oglethorpe decided to go on the offensive and attacked Florida.

His force consisted of 1,000 soldiers from his regiment and the Georgia and South Carolina militia. He also had 1,100 Indian warriors who were willing to fight with him. Oglethorpe's force marched south into Florida in May 1740 and quickly captured a number of smaller outlying forts from the Spanish. However, capturing the massive stone fort at Saint Augustine was more than Oglethorpe and his force were able to do.

The fort that had withstood an earlier attack by South Carolina before Georgia was established had been made even stronger. Oglethorpe decided the only way to capture Saint Augustine was to besiege the fort. Unfortunately, the British naval ships that were a part of the attack were unable to cross the shallow sandbars that guarded the harbor. After 38 days of siege, Oglethorpe was forced to give up. The British ships were threatening to leave as hurricane season would soon be upon them and there were no safe harbors for them in Florida. Also, a number of the troops with Oglethorpe were sick with fever. On July 20, 1740, Oglethorpe and his men packed up and went home.

Two years later, in July 1742, the tables were turned when the Spanish sailed up the coast with a large force and attacked Fort Saint Simon. Oglethorpe and his troops were forced to retreat to Frederica, and the Spanish had a foothold in Georgia. On July 7, 1740, the Spanish tried to take Frederica, but they were held off by Oglethorpe's much smaller force. The Spanish decided to retreat to Fort Saint Simon. However, they stopped along the way to eat.

Oglethorpe had some of his men hidden in the woods along the road to the fort. They waited silently as the Spanish soldiers piled up their rifles and settled down for a meal. They then opened fire and quickly killed, wounded, or captured 500 Spanish soldiers. There was so much blood that it was claimed the water in the nearby marsh turned red. Because of this, the ambush is known as the Battle of Bloody Marsh.

After their defeat at Bloody Marsh and because they thought a British naval force was coming to reinforce Oglethorpe's troops, the Spanish decided to retreat to Florida. The following spring, Oglethorpe tried again to capture Saint Augustine. Despite what he had learned in his first attempt on Saint Augustine, Oglethorpe was no more successful in 1743 than he had been earlier. In July 1743, Oglethorpe sailed to England in hopes of recovering some of the money he had personally used to establish Georgia and answer charges that had been made against him by Lieutenant Colonel William Cooke, a former officer of his troops.

Oglethorpe was successful in both instances. Parliament voted to pay him back more than £66,000. He was also cleared of all charges brought by Cooke. However, his vision for Georgia had never materialized, and he decided to stay in England. He continued to function as one of the trustees until 1749, when he gave that up as well. The original charter for Georgia had granted the trustees only 21 years to establish the colony. As the end of that time approached, it was clear the Crown intended to do as it had done with many other colonies and make Georgia a royal colony.

5

The Royal Colony of Georgia

While Oglethorpe was busy defending the colony from the Spanish, the trustees took steps to arrange a more formal government in Georgia. Although the trustees had made many suggestions and executive orders about the running of their colony, they only really passed three laws for Georgia. One law prohibited the use of strong alcoholic beverages, another prohibited slavery, and the third regulated the Indian trade. The charter gave trustees all the political power in the colony. However, on April 15, 1741, they did divide the colony into two counties—one centered in Savannah and the other at Frederica.

Each county had a president and four assistants appointed by the trustees. The president and assistants were responsible for telling the people what the trustees expected of them. They also ended up hearing a lot of the complaints of the people in the colony. By the end of the War of Jenkins' Ear, many people in Georgia were already thinking that they should have the same rights of self-government as the other 12 British colonies in North America. There were a number of protests against the new form of government.

It was not until 1750 that the trustees finally decided to grant their colonists some say in the governing of the colony. The trustees were already preparing to give the colony back to the Crown as they had no interest in renewing their charter. The colony they had envisioned had never come into being. The repeal

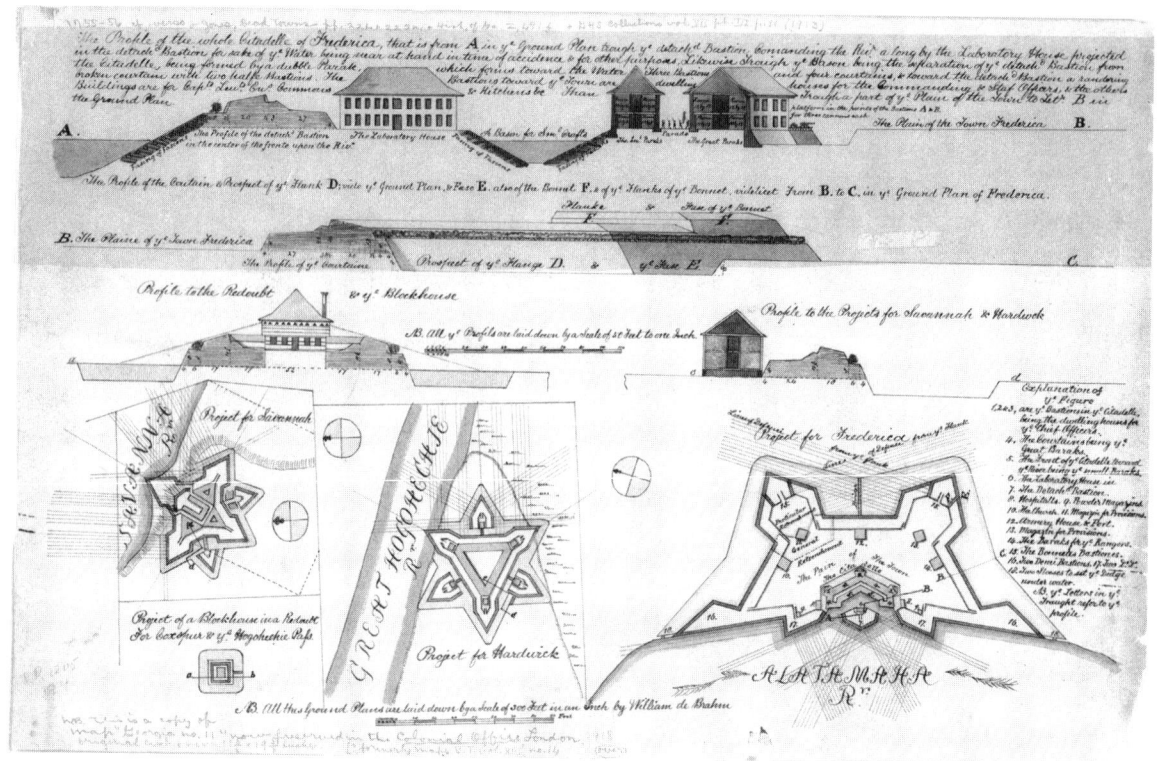

Believed to have been created in 1755, this drawing provides details about Fort Frederica's design and location. *(Courtesy of Hargrett Rare Book & Manuscript Library/University of Georgia Libraries)*

of the ban of slavery probably ensured that it never would. Also, the Crown was unwilling to provide any more money for the Georgia "experiment."

On March 19, 1750, the trustees ordered an election of a colonial assembly with representatives from every community in the colony that had at least 10 families. The role of the assembly would be to make recommendations to the trustees. It had no power to make laws on its own. After elections were held, 16 people from 11 districts came together in Savannah on January 11, 1751, for the first Georgia Assembly. Some of the larger towns, like Savannah, were given more than one representative. Although there were no land requirements to be a representative, most of the people elected owned the 500 acres originally granted to adventurers and were apparently the wealthier people in the colony.

Mary Musgrove Matthews Bosomworth
(ca. 1700–1763)

When Oglethorpe negotiated with the Yamacraw chief Tomochichi for the rights to settle on Yamacraw Bluff, Mary Musgrove (born Coosapakeesa) served as his interpreter. Mary and her husband John Musgrove ran a trading post on the bluff. She was half English and half Creek and spoke both languages fluently. For the next 10 years, Mary helped Oglethorpe in all his dealings with the Creek who even fought with Oglethorpe in his battles against the Spanish. After the death of John Musgrove, Mary married Jacob Matthews, and they ran another trading post at Mount Venture. In 1742, Matthews died, leaving Mary a widow again. When Oglethorpe left the colony, he had promised to make sure that Mary was rewarded for all the help she had provided him in his dealings with the Creek.

To prove his sincerity in rewarding Mary, Oglethorpe gave her £200 and a diamond ring. He also promised her £100 for each year she had served as the colony's interpreter. In 1744, she married her third English husband—Thomas Bosomworth, a Savannah minister. In 1746, Thomas gave up his position as a minister, and he and Mary turned to the business of trading with the Creek. Mary had been a loyal supporter of the colony since it began but was soon upset because she had not been paid the money that Oglethorpe had promised her. Mary and Thomas made their own deals with the Creek and ended up claiming a large amount of land that had been reserved for the Creek.

Once a loyal supporter, Mary soon became a thorn in the side of Georgia. She went so far as to bring a large force of Creek to Savannah to support her claims for back pay and land. In July and August 1749, it looked like there might be fighting in the streets of Savannah. Mary was jailed twice during this period and eventually the Creek went home. It was not until 1760, when Georgia was under the rule of its second royal governor, Henry Ellis, that the Bosomworth's claims were finally settled. In a society dominated by men, Mary Musgrove Matthews Bosomworth played an important role in establishing Georgia. She had proven herself a formidable opponent when she felt she had not been treated fairly.

The Bosomworths led a force to Savannah. *(Courtesy of Hargrett Rare Book & Manuscript Library/University of Georgia Libraries)*

During this first assembly, the representatives drew up a list of requests to be sent to the trustees. The letter that went to the trustees dealt with problems in the colony like the Indian trade and the suggestions that individuals not be allowed to buy land directly from Indians. This may have come about because Mary Musgrove Matthews Bosomworth and her third husband Thomas had negotiated the purchase of a large section of land that had been reserved for the Creek. The assembly also requested practical items such as fire equipment for Savannah, a pilot boat for the Savannah River, and items for soldiers to defend the colony.

What may have been the most important request from the assembly was the right to make laws. The trustees granted almost everything the assembly asked for but flatly refused to give the assembly any control. Part of the reason for this may have been the fact that the trustees had already begun the process of turning the colony over to the Crown. Although the charter granted the trustees authority in the colony for 21 years, they turned it over to the Crown in June 1752—one year early. There never was a second Georgia Assembly under the trustees. As a royal colony, Georgia was given a whole new form of government.

ROYAL GOVERNMENT

As a royal colony, a government was established for Georgia that mirrored that of most of the other American colonies. The real power in the colony was held by the royal governor, who was appointed by the king. Georgia's first royal governor was John Reynolds. As royal governor, Reynolds was both the political and military leader of the colony. He had complete control over just about every aspect of the colony. He was the only one who could grant new land to colonists. He also was in charge of the courts. The charter called for a legislative branch but that, too, was controlled by the governor.

The legislature was set up with two houses. Members of the upper house were appointed by the king at the recommendation of the governor, and they were intended to advise the governor. The lower house was known as the Commons House. It was made up of elected representatives from the newly divided parishes in the colony. Representatives to the Commons House had to be men who owned at least 500 acres. Any adult male who owned at least

John Reynolds ruled Georgia as the colony's first royal governor. This portrait of Reynolds by South Carolina colonist Jeremiah Theus was probably painted during Reynolds's tenure as governor. *(National Maritime Museum, London)*

50 acres was allowed to vote for a representative from the parish in which he lived.

This system rarely worked well in any of the colonies, and Georgia was no exception. Governor Reynolds ruled as a dictator and had little or no regard for the elected representatives of the people. The members of the Commons House complained repeatedly to London about Reynolds, and he was soon replaced.

The French and Indian Wars
(ca. 1689–1762)

Between 1689 and 1762, France and Great Britain went to war four times. The first three wars were fought primarily in Europe although they created conflicts between the French and English colonies in North America. The first three were known in North America by the name of the king or queen of England at the time of the war. They were:

> King William's War (1689–1697)
> Queen Anne's War (1702–1713)
> King George's War (1744–1748)

The fourth war was fought over who would control North America and is known as the French and Indian War. The name comes from the fact that the French were joined by many Indian allies in all four of the wars, which were fought primarily along the border between New France (now Canada) and the English colonies in the Northeast.

However, before the fourth war, the French attempted to link their colonies in the north with their colony in Louisiana. Forts were built along the Mississippi River and in western Pennsylvania along the upper reaches of the Ohio River. It was in the wilderness of Pennsylvania that most of the fighting took place during the French and Indian War. In the early years of the war, it looked like the French were going to win.

Although no fighting occurred in Georgia, the fact that the French were to their west and were competing directly with Indian traders from Georgia caused concern for many. The Georgians were afraid that the French and Indian War might spread to the Georgian frontier. This slowed growth in the colony in the years immediately following Georgia becoming a royal colony. The war ended in 1762, and Great Britain received all the land east of the Mississippi River and what would become Canada. By 1760, it was clear to most people that Britain would win the French and Indian War, and Georgia entered a period of growth and prosperity that continued until the American Revolution.

However, the system of government for a royal colony left little room for the people to feel that it was their government. Even as Georgia began to prosper under royal control, many in the colony already wanted more say in their own affairs.

Reynolds was replaced by Henry Ellis on February 16, 1757. Ellis stayed in Georgia as governor for three years and under his able leadership the turmoil caused by Reynolds disappeared. The political situation in Georgia remained relatively calm until Parliament turned to the colonies to raise revenue to pay off the debts it had built up during the last of the French and Indian wars (1755–62).

One benefit of being a royal colony was rapid growth. By 1760, the almost 10,000 people who lived in Georgia were still living along the Savannah River and the coast. Of Georgia's four largest modern-day cities, Atlanta, Columbus, Macon, and Augusta, only Augusta was established before the 1800s. In the time between 1760 and the start of the American Revolution in 1775, Georgia grew rapidly. The original land of the colony that had been agreed on with the Creek was a strip 50 miles inland from the Savannah River and the tidewater, including the islands between the Savannah and Altamaha Rivers. The tidewater area is considered the land from the coast inland to what is known as the fall line. The fall line is the point on a river of the first rapids or waterfall. During the colonial period, many oceangoing ships were small enough to sail far upriver, and many plantations had their own docks where they could ship out their crops.

By the early 1760s, the tidewater and the lands along the Savannah River had been filled. Officials in the colony knew they had to get more land from the Creek if the colony was going to continue to grow. In fall 1763, a meeting was held at Augusta between colonial and Creek leaders. The result of this meeting was the Treaty of Augusta, which was signed on November 10, 1763. In this treaty, the Creek gave up 2.4 million acres to white settlement. This included the tidewater between the Altamaha and Saint Marys Rivers, as well as land north of Augusta to the Little River. It also expanded the area available to settlement along the Savannah River west to the Ogeechee River.

This additional land was extremely important to Georgia, which had established agricultural practices similar to South Carolina. The mulberry trees and silk worms imported to the colony by the trustees had not adapted to Georgia's climate and soil conditions. When the farmers of Georgia turned to rice and indigo (a plant that was used to make blue dye), they started being successful. Just about everyone in Georgia was involved in agriculture to some extent. Even people in towns like Savannah had farms outside town where they grew at least some of their own food.

Like other southern colonies, the farmers in Georgia were divided socially by the amount of land they owned. There were a

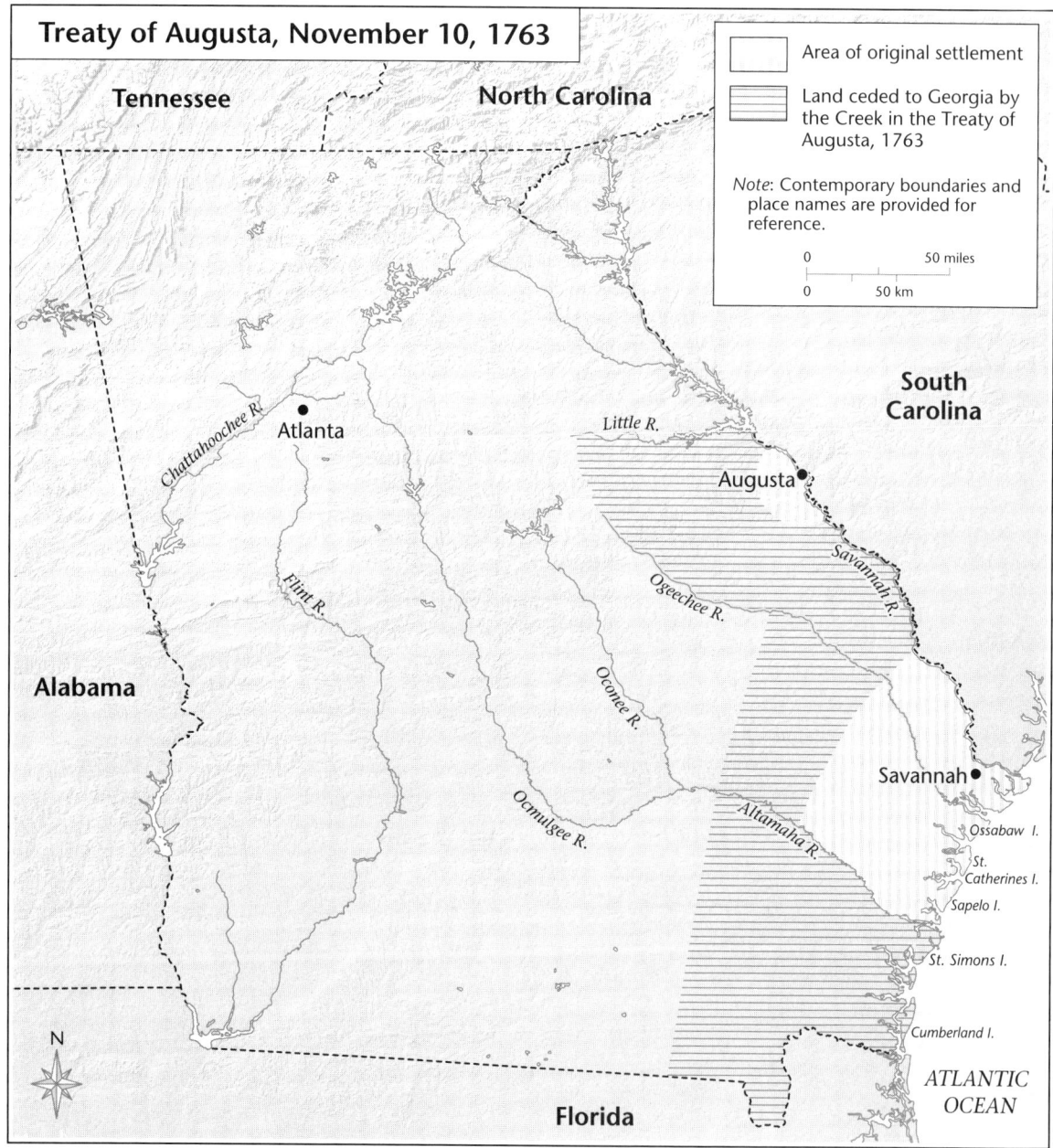

The Treaty of Augusta was negotiated by officials in Georgia with the Creek and greatly increased the land available for settlement by colonists.

small number of landowners—many of whom also owned plantations in South Carolina—who had large plantations worked by numerous slaves. The majority of the people in the colony owned medium-size farms that they worked themselves or with the help of a couple of slaves or indentured servants. At the time, Georgia also had a large number of poor farmers. Almost one-third of the people in the colony lived on small farms and had no slaves or servants. These farmers found it difficult to grow enough food to feed their families. The small farms of Georgia were located along the frontier and belonged to people who had arrived in the colony as charity colonists or indentured servants. They had been granted only 50 acres, and they were usually of poorer quality than the tidewater or the land closer to the Savannah River.

The people who came to Georgia in the first 40 years of the colony came from all over. Approximately two-thirds of the whites in Georgia were of English descent. However, many of these people came to Georgia from other colonies. The rest of the whites in the colony came from countries in Europe as well as from Ireland and Scotland. By this time, the slave population of Georgia had grown substantially as well.

Although the official church of the colony was the Church of England, the people who settled in Georgia brought a wide variety of religious beliefs with them. All of the various Protestant groups were tolerated, and Georgia was more tolerant of Jews than most of the other American colonies. However, Catholics were not allowed in Georgia. England was officially a Protestant country, and its main enemies, France and Spain, were both Catholic countries. This continued to fuel anti-Catholic feelings in Great Britain and its colonies and was one of the underlying causes of the French and Indian wars.

After the French and Indian War, Parliament was faced with huge debts from the war. The Crown was also faced with the increased costs of administering the lands it had taken from the French in North America. Although there were few people in 1763 in the thirteen original English colonies thinking about independence, the attempts by the Crown to tax the colonies would lead to war 12 years later.

6

The Road to Revolution

Third royal governor of Georgia, James Wright ruled the colony from 1760 until 1782. *(Courtesy of Hargrett Rare Book & Manuscript Library/University of Georgia Libraries)*

In the time between the end of the French and Indian War in 1763 and the start of fighting at the Battles of Lexington and Concord in 1775, people in the colonies reacted differently to the growing protests against the Crown. Massachusetts and Virginia were the colonies with the strongest anti-British feelings. Massachusetts was the place where the first fighting between British soldiers and colonial militiamen took place. Georgia often reacted more slowly and less strongly to the various taxes that drove people in other colonies to take up arms against the Crown.

There were a number of reasons for Georgia to be on the edge of the rebellion. The fact that Georgia was the farthest away from the centers of the protest played a part in its often lukewarm reactions. In addition, Georgia's royal governor during the time, James Wright, was an efficient leader who had come to the colony in 1760. During his time in office, Governor Wright oversaw the

Loyalists versus Patriots

When the American Revolution started in 1775, it has been estimated that the people in the colonies were fairly evenly divided. One-third of the people were believed to consider themselves Patriots and were in favor of breaking away from the Crown. Another third were Loyalists who wanted to stay a part of the British Empire. The remaining third were neutral. In places like Boston, the Patriots had the upper hand, while in Georgia, the Loyalists seemed to hold control longer. After the fighting began, more and more people chose sides. Many Loyalists left the colonies for Canada, England, or another place where they could be safe from attack. In Georgia and some of the other colonies, Loyalists organized and attacked their Patriot neighbors.

time of greatest growth and prosperity for the youngest of the colonies. Virginia, Massachusetts, and some of the other colonies were more than 100 years older than Georgia, and their citizens felt little, if any, ties with England.

Many of the settlers in Georgia had been born in England and still thought of themselves as British. Of the thirteen colonies, Georgia was the colony with the highest percentage of Loyalists (people loyal to the king). Eventually, though, the Patriots in Georgia would lead the colony in joining the other 12 colonies and becoming part of the United States.

In the peace following the French and Indian War, Parliament was faced with an immense debt. It seemed logical to leaders in London that the people in North America pay a fair share of the debt. They were the ones who benefited the most from the removal of the French from their borders. They also paid much less in the way of taxes than people in England. One of the reasons that the colonies did not produce enough revenue for the Crown was because of all the illegal trade that went on.

The Crown passed many laws regulating trade in its colonies. Goods were only supposed to be traded between the colonies and Great Britain. However, almost from the beginning, merchants in the English colonies began trading outside the British mercantile system. They found that sugar from French and Spanish plantations

Many British colonies in the Caribbean produced sugar from sugarcane. In this mid-18th-century British engraving, a white overseer directs some Native peoples (possibly in the West Indies) while they process sugarcane. *(Library of Congress, Prints and Photographs Division [LC-USZ62-7841])*

in the Caribbean was cheaper than the sugar from British-controlled islands. Much of the wealth in the colonies, especially in the Northeast, came from this illegal trade.

As Parliament looked around for ways to raise money to pay down its debt, they first focused on the illegal trade in sugar and molasses. One of the major industries in New England was the manufacture of rum, an alcoholic beverage distilled from molasses. Parliament passed the Sugar Act of 1764 in hopes of cleaning up the illegal trade and raising revenue. The law actually lowered the taxes on legally imported sugar and molasses. However, it attempted to make it much harder for New England merchants to smuggle in illegal molasses and sugar. There were some protests from the merchants in New England over the Sugar Act, but its impact was not that great. However, that was not the case with Parliament's next attempt at taxing the colonies.

THE STAMP ACT (March 22, 1765)

When the Sugar Act failed to produce much in the way of additional revenue for the Crown, George Grenville, Britain's first minister, came up with another plan. He suggested a Stamp Act for the American colonies, and Parliament passed it on March 22, 1765. This law required that all legal documents, printed

The Road to Revolution

When affixed to goods, this stamp signified that a tax had been paid upon purchase. Many colonists felt that the British unfairly introduced these taxes when they implemented the Stamp Act in 1765, which affected goods ranging from business transactions to playing cards. *(Library of Congress, Prints and Photographs Division [LC-USZ61-539])*

materials, licenses, ships' papers, cards, dice, and a number of other items have an official stamp attached to them. The stamps had to be bought from the Crown's stamp agent in each colony and affixed to the item before the transaction would be legal.

The idea of a stamp tax was not new. Stamp taxes existed in England at the time and had even been used by some of the colonies in North America. The reaction to the Stamp Act was more about the relationship between the colonies and Parliament. Some people in the colonies believed that it was not right to be taxed by Parliament because it had no representatives from the colonies. The cry of "No taxation without representation" was heard throughout the colonies. Radical groups of Patriots known as the Sons of Liberty organized into often secret groups to lead the protests.

The Stamp Act was passed in March and scheduled to go into effect on November 1, 1765. As the time approached to start using the stamps, the protests grew more vocal and

The Sons of Liberty

When the Stamp Act was passed by Parliament in 1765, people in the colonies formed groups in their communities to protest the act. One of the opponents of the Stamp Act in the House of Commons in Parliament, Isaac Barré, called the protesters the "sons of liberty." Soon the name spread to the colonies, where it was readily adopted. It was the various Sons of Liberty groups that organized protests against the Stamp Act and later held "tea parties" in places like Boston, New Jersey, and South Carolina when the Tea Act of 1773 was passed. Although there was a Sons of Liberty group in Georgia, its membership was small and secret. Governor Wright referred to them as "Liberty Boys," and they were often joined by radicals from South Carolina when there were public protests in Savannah.

The Stamp Act Congress
(October 1766)

When the Stamp Act passed Parliament, the Massachusetts assembly sent out what was called a circular letter. It went to Patriot leaders and assemblies in all the colonies. The Massachusetts circular letter called for the colonies to send representatives to a congress in October 1767 in New York City to discuss what to do about the Stamp Act. Nine colonies sent representatives. New Hampshire did not send any representatives but sent a letter of support for the actions the congress might take. In Virginia, North Carolina, and Georgia, the royal governors refused to call the assembly into session to select delegates to the congress. The Stamp Act Congress sent a petition to the king and Parliament that explained that the colonies believed Parliament had the right to pass laws that affected them but did not have the right to pass taxes. They believed that right belonged to the legislature in each colony.

sometimes violent. In some places, houses and/or businesses of the stamp agents were damaged or destroyed. There were protests against the Stamp Act in Savannah. In October 1765, just before the

Colonists denounce the Stamp Act in 1765. *(Library of Congress)*

The Road to Revolution

The first newspaper in Georgia, *The Georgia Gazette* began publication in 1763. Its publication was suspended from November 1765 until May 1766 as a result of the Stamp Act. Shown here is an image of the front page of the January 12, 1774, issue. *(Georgia Historical Society)*

Stamp Act was to go into effect, a large crowd paraded dummies dressed as British officials through the streets and then burned them.

Many of the stamp agents resigned rather than face the anger of the mobs stirred up by the Sons of Liberty. In Georgia, the stamp agent was George Angus, and he was the only stamp agent in all the colonies who came directly from England. Angus did not arrive in the colony until January 3, 1766. Up until that time, no stamps had been issued. The only newspaper in the colony, the *Georgia Gazette* had shut down for lack of stamps. A number of ships were kept in port because they could not get stamps on their ship's papers. On January 7, 1766, Angus opened for business in the governor's house and began selling stamps so the ships stuck in the harbor could leave.

As it turned out, the stamps that Angus sold in January were the only stamps sold in any of the colonies. After clearing a number of ships from Savannah, Angus felt pressured to stop selling stamps, and he moved out of Savannah. In March, he left Georgia and was never heard from again. Governor Wright had the remaining stamps locked up to keep them safe. Then, on February 2, 1766, he had the stamps put on the British naval ship *Speedwell* for safekeeping. The stamps were never returned to Georgia, and the Stamp Act was repealed on March 18, 1766.

However, Parliament also passed the Declaratory Act at the same time. The Declaratory Act made it clear that they believed they had the right to pass whatever laws they saw fit—including taxes—for the American colonies. The repeal of the Stamp Act ended most of the protest in the colonies for the time being. Then, a little more than a year later, Parliament decided to try again and passed the Townshend Duties.

THE TOWNSHEND DUTIES
(June 29, 1767)

The failure of the Sugar and Stamp Acts made the financial situation for the Crown even worse. In addition, Parliament had cut the taxes in England by £500,000 to give some relief to the people there. One of the complaints against the Stamp Act was that it was a direct tax on the people in the colonies. Benjamin

Franklin, who served as the London agent for his home colony of Pennsylvania and later for Georgia, told Parliament that the direct tax of the Stamp Act was the main problem. He felt that an indirect tax, like a duty on imports, would be more acceptable in the colonies.

Following the advice of Franklin and others, Charles Townshend proposed a series of duties on some of the items that the colonies imported from Britain. These duties were passed on June 29, 1767, and taxed the importation of glass, lead, painter's color, paper, and tea. These are usually referred to as the Townshend Duties. At first, the people in the colonies did not know how to react to the Townshend Duties. However, over the next few years the Patriots were able to come to an agreement with merchants and their customers not to import or sell any of the goods included in the Townshend Duties.

Massachusetts issued another circular letter calling for everyone to participate in the boycott of British goods. Then, the ship *Liberty*, which belonged to John Hancock was seized in Boston for trying to bring goods into Boston without paying the duty. The Sons of Liberty and their Patriot followers staged a number of demonstrations in Boston, and the British decided to send troops to the city. There were also British troops in New York City. Rather than calm things down, the troops only served to anger the Patriots. In New York City, off-duty British soldiers were taking jobs away from American laborers. The soldiers and workers clashed on January 18, 1770, in what is known as the Battle of Golden Hill. Although no one was killed, a number of people on both sides were injured.

Three months later in Boston, a confrontation between a mob of protesters and British soldiers had a deadly outcome. On March 5, 1770, a young Patriot shouted insults at a soldier in front of the Boston customshouse. The soldier took offense and hit the young man in the head with his musket. The boy ran off and told people what had happened. Soon there were more than 400 angry people in front of the customshouse, and more soldiers were called to the scene.

The crowd shouted at the soldiers and threw chunks of ice and snowballs at the soldiers. As the soldiers grew more tense, they loaded their guns. Nobody knows who, but someone yelled

Paul Revere's engraving of the Boston Massacre depicts the event that many consider the beginning of the struggle for independence. It occurred on March 5, 1770. *(Library of Congress, Prints and Photographs Division [LC-USZ62-35522])*

"fire." When the smoke cleared from the British muskets, three Patriots were dead in the street and two others were wounded and would die later. This event is known as the Boston Massacre, and it served to rally even more people against the Crown. By this time, Parliament had decided to give up on the Townshend Duties, and all but the tax on tea were repealed in April 1770. Keeping the tax on tea was more symbolic than anything else. Parliament did not want to give in completely to the protests in the colonies. With the repeal of the Townshend Duties, the situation in the colonies quieted down and had Parliament not interfered again, the thirteen American colonies might still be a part of the British Commonwealth like Canada and Australia.

THE TEA ACT
(May 10, 1773)

The British East India Company had the exclusive rights to bring tea from Asia to Great Britain. Many wealthy and influential people, including a number of members of Parliament, owned stock in the company. In the early 1770s, it looked like the company was going to go through bankruptcy. The system by which all tea had to be brought to England and sold to wholesalers who then exported it to other wholesalers in the colonies made English tea very expensive. It also limited the profits of the East India Company.

To save the company, Parliament passed what is known as the Tea Act on May 10, 1773. The Tea Act eliminated the middlemen and allowed the company to directly ship tea to the American colonies. This would have made tea actually cheaper in the colonies, while at the same time allowing the company to make more money. No one in England thought there would be any objections in the colonies. However, the company was given a monopoly on tea sales in America, and this angered many.

When tea arrived in Boston Harbor, a group from the Sons of Liberty slightly disguised themselves as Indians and went aboard

To protest the passage of the Tea Act, some male colonists, disguised as American Indians, boarded three ships in Boston Harbor on December 16, 1773, and dumped hundreds of cases of tea into the harbor. The event became known as the Boston Tea Party. *(Library of Congress)*

the ships carrying the tea. Without hurting anyone and without damaging the ships, £10,000 worth of tea was dumped into Boston Harbor. During the next year, similar incidents occurred in New York City; Annapolis, Maryland; and elsewhere in the colonies. Although there was not much reaction to what is known as the Boston Tea Party in Georgia, the reaction of Parliament did more to upset Patriots in Georgia and throughout the colonies.

THE INTOLERABLE ACTS (1774)

In response to the Boston Tea Party, Parliament was directed by the government led by Frederick, Lord North to punish the people in the colonies. Parliament passed a series of five laws in 1774 that they referred to as the Coercive Acts. In the colonies, they were known as the Intolerable Acts. The most threatening to all the colonies were the first two acts. The first was called the Boston Port Bill, and it closed Boston Harbor to all shipping until the tea that had been dumped in the harbor was paid for. The second was known as the Massachusetts Government Act. This law changed the Massachusetts charter, taking power away from the elected officials in the colony and giving it to the Crown.

Patriots in Georgia and throughout the colonies were very upset by the Intolerable Acts. They rightly believed that if the Crown could do this to Massachusetts, it could do the same to any of the colonies at any time. On July 27, 1774, the Patriots in Savannah held a general meeting at a liberty pole erected outside Tondee's Tavern, a known meeting place for the colony's Patriots.

At this meeting, numerous resolutions and letters from Massachusetts and the other colonies were read. They also called for a statewide meeting to be held in Savannah on August 10. Every parish in the colony sent representatives to the August meeting. The representatives at this meeting came up with a series of resolutions supporting the Patriots in Boston and throughout the colonies.

In response to this meeting, Governor Wright had petitions circulated and got more than 600 signatures from people who claimed to still be loyal to the king. When Wright's petitions were published in the *Georgia Gazette*, the Patriots went out and circulated

Liberty Poles and Trees

Throughout the colonies, the Sons of Liberty designated meeting places. These were often outdoors under the spreading limbs of a tree or marked by a decorated pole, called a liberty pole. The trees became known as Liberty Trees. The one in Boston, Massachusetts, was a giant elm that was cut down by British soldiers during the Siege of Boston in 1775. It supposedly yielded 14 cords of firewood. The Liberty Tree in Charleston, South Carolina, was an oak. When the city was captured by the British in 1780, they cut down the tree and then burned the stump. The Patriots of Charleston dug up the roots of the Liberty Tree and made canes of them. Reportedly, Thomas Jefferson was presented with a cane from the roots of the Charleston Liberty Tree. The last remaining Liberty Tree from the time of the American Revolution was a huge poplar on the campus of St. John's College in Annapolis, Maryland. Over the years, people went to great lengths to keep the tree alive. It was finally cut down in 1999 after it was severely damaged by a hurricane.

The last remaining Liberty Tree, shown here on the campus of St. John's College in Annapolis, Maryland, in a 1906 photograph, stood until 1999. *(Library of Congress, Prints and Photographs Division [LC-D4-19117])*

their own petitions. The major impact of the opposing petitions was to show how deeply divided the people of Georgia were.

The Georgia Patriots failed to answer a call from Massachusetts and some of the other colonies to send delegates to a Continental Congress in 1774. The idea of sending delegates was debated at the August meeting but not acted upon. As it turned out, Georgia was the only colony not represented at what is called the First Continental Congress.

THE FIRST CONTINENTAL CONGRESS (1774)

The delegates to the First Continental Congress met in Philadelphia, Pennsylvania, from September 5 to October 26, 1774. The main action of the congress was to call for a general boycott of all English goods. Delegates also condemned the Intolerable Acts and made up a list of complaints to be sent to the king. The First Continental Congress showed that the colonies could work together to solve the problems they faced. As a final act, the representatives agreed to meet for a Second Continental Congress in the spring

The First Continental Congress met in Philadelphia and composed and sent resolutions to the king of Britain. A second congress was planned for the following spring, to assess the situation. *(Library of Congress, Prints and Photographs Division [LC-USZ62-45328])*

and assess any progress that might have been made by that time. However, before the Second Continental Congress could convene, the situation in Massachusetts went from bad to worse as fighting broke out in April between the colonial militia and British troops at the Battles of Lexington and Concord.

7

The War for Independence

THE WAR STARTS IN THE NORTH

After the passage of the Intolerable Acts, the situation in Massachusetts became increasingly tense. Throughout the colonies, local militia began drilling and stockpiling weapons and ammunition. Most people hoped that there could still be a peaceful settlement of the problems between the Crown and the colonies. However, the First Continental Congress had suggested that the militia start preparing just in case the situation turned violent.

In April 1775, General Thomas Gage, the commander of the British forces in Boston received orders that allowed him to move against the Patriots who were organizing outside the city. On the night of April 18, 1775, 800 British soldiers, called "redcoats" by the Patriots because of the color of their uniform coats, slipped out of Boston across Back Bay. They were headed toward Lexington and Concord, Massachusetts. Patriots watched the redcoats leave the city and then raised a signal in the Old North Church in Boston to alert riders to the soldiers' route. They had decided that one lantern would mean the soldiers were going overland, and two lanterns would mean they were using boats.

When the two-lantern signal was put up in the church's steeple, Paul Revere and other Patriots rode out into the night to warn the militia. By the time the redcoats arrived in Lexington on the morning of April 19, they found 70 local militiamen waiting

The night of April 18, 1775, Paul Revere completed his midnight ride during which he warned colonists that the British were heading inland from Boston. *(Library of Congress)*

for them. The British officer ordered the militia to drop their rifles and surrender. Instead, the militiamen tried to escape, and a shot was fired. No one knows who fired that first shot. In response, the

British soldiers fired two volleys at the scattering Patriots. Eight Patriots were killed and 10 others wounded.

The redcoats then headed for Concord, where they believed a supply of munitions was stored. When they reached the North Bridge in Concord, a much larger Patriot force was waiting for them. The British sustained casualties in the battle and decided to retreat. It was during the retreat to Boston that the British were hit the hardest. Thousands of militia from the area came to join the fight. They repeatedly ambushed the redcoats as they tried to get back to the relative safety of Boston. Fortunately for the British soldiers, General Gage sent out 2,000 soldiers to help them fight their way back to the city. As it was, the British lost 273 men who were killed, wounded, or missing. On the Patriot side, the losses were about one-third that number.

Word of the Battles of Lexington and Concord spread quickly through the colonies. Militia units from all over the Northeast rushed to Boston and soon had the city surrounded. The hopes of many for a peaceful settlement between the colonies and the Crown ended as they realized that war had begun. It took until May 10, 1775, for news of the battles to reach Savannah. The Patriots in the town broke into the governor's powder magazine the next night and stole the gunpowder stored there. They also jammed spikes into 21 cannons along the bluff that were there to protect the water approach to Savannah. The spiked cannons were then pushed over the edge of the bluff. The powder was used by both the Georgia and South Carolina militia. It has been reported that some of the powder even made it to Boston and the Battle of Bunker Hill on June 17, 1775.

GEORGIA JOINS THE REVOLUTION

When Georgia did not send delegates to the First Continental Congress, a resolution was passed calling on the other 12 colonies not to trade with Georgia. With the beginning of fighting, Georgia Patriots wanted to be sure they were a part of the rebellion. They had held a Provincial Congress on January 17, 1775. However, they failed to gain the support of the Commons House, accomplishing little. When the Second Provincial Congress came together on July 4, 1775, at Tondee's Tavern in Savannah, it was clear that they were ready to split the colony into Patriots and Loyalists.

Lyman Hall served as a Georgia delegate at the Second Continental Congress and signed the Declaration of Independence on the colony's behalf. Hall was governor of Georgia in 1783. *(Courtesy of Hargrett Rare Book & Manuscript Library/University of Georgia Libraries)*

They appointed five men to be delegates to the Second Continental Congress: Archibald Bulloch, Lyman Hall, John Houstoun, Noble W. Jones, and Reverend John J. Zubly. Governor Wright was still in Savannah, but even he felt that the Patriots were in control of the colony. At this time, Governor Wright wrote to London asking for permission to return to England. Six months later, he left the colony and did not return until it was captured by British forces in 1778.

In the early years of the American Revolution, most of the fighting was in the North. After George Washington was named commander of the newly formed Continental army, he was able to drive the British out of Boston. He then turned his attention to taking New York away from the British. The New York campaign was a disaster for the Patriots. The British chased Washington out

Georgia Delegates Elected to the Second Continental Congress
(July 1775)

The election of Archibald Bulloch, Lyman Hall, John Houstoun, Noble W. Jones, and Reverend John J. Zubly to the Second Continental Congress made Georgia a full partner with the other 12 colonies in the rebellion against the Crown. The personal history of these five men tells a lot about the Patriots in Georgia. Only one of the five was born in England. Archibald Bulloch grew up in Charleston, South Carolina, and had moved to Georgia in 1750. Lyman Hall was born in Connecticut and had graduated from Yale before moving to South Carolina with a group of Puritans. Many from this group moved to Midway, Georgia in 1752. John Houstoun was the only one of the five born in Georgia. His father had been a leader in the colonial government of Georgia. Noble W. Jones had come to Georgia as a small child on the *Ann*. John Zubly was born in Switzerland and had lived in South Carolina before coming to Georgia. All five of these men, like most Patriots, had little if any ties to England and considered themselves Georgians and Americans.

Declaring Independence
(1776)

On April 15, 1776, the Georgia Provincial Congress adopted a temporary constitution known as the Rules and Regulations of 1776. This created an independent state government with a single house legislature and a weak executive branch. On June 12, the Provincial Congress made it clear that they intended to join with the other colonies in seeking justice. When the Continental Congress voted to declare independence in July 1776, Georgia's delegates voted in favor of independence. In an informal poll of the delegations, two states were against independence. Pennsylvania and South Carolina delegations said they would vote against. Pennsylvania's delegation included one representative who was against the war but for independence. When he left the congress, Pennsylvania said it would vote in favor of independence even if it meant the war would continue.

(continues)

Representing Georgia at the Second Continental Congress, Button Gwinnett signed the Declaration of Independence. Gwinnett died one year later from wounds he suffered in a duel with Lachlan McIntosh resulting from political differences. *(Georgia Historical Society)*

George Walton represented Georgia at the Second Continental Congress and signed the Declaration of Independence on the colony's behalf. At 26, he was the youngest person to sign that document. *(Courtesy of Hargrett Rare Book & Manuscript Library/University of Georgia Libraries)*

(continued)

At this point, South Carolina said it would join with the rest. New York did not vote in the first formal count so it was 12 to zero in favor of independence. New York joined the other states a few days later to make it unanimous. On July 4, 1776, another vote was taken to accept the Declaration of Independence that had primarily been written by Thomas Jefferson of Virginia. After approving the declaration, the delegates later signed the original document. The signers for Georgia were Button Gwinnett, Lyman Hall, and George Walton. The document they signed opens with the following paragraph:

When in the Course of human events, it becomes necessary for one people to dissolve the political bands which have connected them with another, and to assume among the Powers of the earth, the separate and equal station to which the Laws of Nature and of Nature's God entitle them, a decent respect to opinions of mankind requires that they should declare the causes which impel them to the separation.

of New York and across New Jersey. Had Washington not crossed the Delaware River into Pennsylvania and made sure there were no boats left for the British to use to follow him, the war might have ended in 1776 with the British winning. As it turned out, Washington was able to avoid large battles with the better-equipped and -trained British forces until the Continental army was defeated at the Battle of Brandywine in Pennsylvania on September 11, 1777.

After defeating Washington, the British easily captured the Patriot capital of Philadelphia. Washington and his forces spent a terrible winter at Valley Forge, Pennsylvania. Two events changed the course of the war. In fall 1777, the French decided to enter the war on the side of the Patriots, and the British command in England decided that it might be a better strategy to move the war to the South. Royal governors Wright of Georgia and Lord William Campbell of South Carolina had convinced officials in London that their former colonies were home to many Loyalists who would rally to the British if they invaded.

In the years before the British turned their full attention to the South, there had been only sporadic fighting in Georgia. On March 2, 1776, Georgia Patriots and British forces fought for control of a number of ships in Savannah that were loaded with rice. The Patri-

One of the first and boldest acts of the Second Continental Congress was to compose and sign the Declaration of Independence in summer 1776. *(Library of Congress)*

ots were able to burn some of the ships, but the British escaped with some of the others and took 1,600 barrels of rice that were used to feed British troops in the North.

After the French and Indian War, Florida had become British territory, and there was raiding on both sides of the border. A group of Loyalists, many of them from Georgia, formed what was called the Florida Rangers and frequently raided Georgia. They stole cattle and burned farms, and then slipped back into Florida before Patriot forces could catch them. During this same time, Patriot leaders attempted three different times to mount campaigns against Florida and hoped to capture Saint Augustine. For a number of reasons, they were no more successful than Oglethorpe had been during the War of Jenkins' Ear. There were also a number of reported attacks by Patriots on those believed to be Loyalists in Georgia.

THE WAR COMES TO GEORGIA

Georgia had fewer than 4,000 adult males in the colony. If a large number of them had gone off to fight in the Continental army, many in Georgia would have suffered. Most of those from Georgia who participated in the Revolution did so as members of local troops. In fact, Georgia repeatedly requested troops from the Continental Congress to defend its border with Florida and to protect Savannah. However, General Washington was hard pressed to put enough soldiers in the field at any given time and refused to send soldiers to Georgia.

The new plan that was decided upon in London called for British troops to fall back to New York City in the North and then turn their attention to Georgia. They believed that if they captured Georgia they could then fight their way north through the South. The goal was to eventually capture Virginia, which was considered the center of the rebellion.

In November 1778, the first attacks by regular British forces against Georgia began. Their first attack was on the fort of Sunbury, Georgia. It has been reported that the Patriot in charge of the fort, Colonel John McIntosh, defied the British. When they demanded he surrender the fort he said, "Come and take it!" For the time being, the British decided not to commit to a siege of the fort and left until they could come back with a larger force.

Word reached Georgia that a large British force from New York was headed south to take Savannah. The knowledge of the pending invasion seems to have been ignored by the Patriots in Savannah. However, with a force of only 600 to defend the town, there may have been little that they could do. Late in December 1778, the British force from New York arrived off the coast of Georgia. On December 29, they landed a large force of several thousand soldiers below Savannah without opposition from the Patriots. The British were able to march directly into town where they captured 450 militiamen. Another 100 men were killed or drowned in the swamps outside Savannah as they tried to escape the British.

As 1778 came to an end, Georgia was once again under the control of the British. The Loyalist support that the British received was never equal to what had been promised by Wright and others. But they were soon in control of most of the state. More than 1,400 men took oaths of loyalty to the king, but some have suggested that many only did it so they could keep their homes and other property. In July 1779, Governor Wright returned to Georgia to continue where he had left off. Although the two sides continued to fight for control of what is referred to as up-country—that part of the state inland from the coast and above Augusta on the Savannah River—the British held onto Savannah until July 1782.

The Patriots, along with a fleet of French ships commanded by Count Jean-Baptiste-Charles-Henri-Hector d'Estaing, did make one attempt to recapture Savannah in fall 1779. General Benjamin Lincoln brought 2,000 Continental soldiers to the outskirts of Savannah by land and Count d'Estaing arrived by sea. When the British in Savannah realized the size of the force facing them they asked for a day to think about surrendering. Unfortunately, Count d'Estaing agreed to this delay. While the French waited for the surrender of Savannah, the British

A general in the Continental army, Benjamin Lincoln led a force of 2,000 soldiers to Savannah to try to recapture Georgia from the British, who had seized control of the colony. *(Library of Congress, Prints and Photographs Division [LC-USZ62-45245])*

The War for Independence

Nancy Hart

One of the legends to come out of the fighting in Georgia was the story of Nancy Hart. It has been passed down that sometime in 1780, a group of Loyalist fighters stopped at the farm of Patriots Captain Benjamin Hart and his wife Nancy in Wilkes County in northeastern Georgia. Nancy Hart was at home with her daughter, and the Loyalists demanded that she feed them. They stacked their rifles in a corner and sat down at the table. As they talked about having just killed the Patriot leader John Dooly, Nancy sent her daughter to fetch her father and any other men he could bring.

Nancy fed the men, and as they ate and drank she kept sneaking over to their rifles and sliding them out of the cabin through a crack in the wall. When one of the men noticed what she was doing, he rushed her. The unflappable heroine took one of the remaining rifles and shot and killed him. She then grabbed another rifle and wounded the next man who made a move toward her. At this point, Captain Hart and a group of his neighbors burst into the cabin and captured the remaining Loyalists. The story continues that Captain Hart wanted to shoot the remaining Loyalists, but Nancy convinced them that hanging them would be more appropriate.

Located in Elbert County, Georgia, the log cabin that Nancy and Benjamin Hart lived in during the Revolutionary War was reconstructed by the Elbert County Daughters of the American Revolution in the 1930s and included some of the stones from the original chimney. *(Image courtesy of Scott Sutherland)*

strengthened their defenses and 1,000 more troops arrived from South Carolina.

On October 4, 1779, the French fleet began bombarding Savannah. Although they did substantial damage to the town, the British had dug in and were ready for them when the French and American soldiers finally attacked on October 9. D'Estaing personally led the charge into the city, but his forces were stopped by the British, and the count was wounded. Rather than mounting a siege of the city, d'Estaing decided to leave on October 20. Without the French, the Continental forces did not stand a chance, and they also withdrew, leaving Savannah to the British.

During the time that the British controlled Savannah, there was constant fighting between Loyalist and Patriot forces in the upcountry. Often these were small forces that raided the farms of people believed to be on the other side.

For over a year during the occupation of Georgia, the Patriot state government remained in hiding and may have met in a variety of places, including across the Savannah River in South Carolina. On May 12, 1780, the British captured Charleston, South Carolina, and it looked like their southern strategy was working. Continental troops harassed the British as they fought their way north into Virginia but could not stop them. By October, General Lord Cornwallis had made it all the way to Yorktown on the shore of Chesapeake Bay. But this was as far as he would get. The French navy blocked any reinforcements from reaching him by sea, and a combined force of French and Continental soldiers surrounded his position. By mid-October, Lord Cornwallis knew his position was hopeless. He surrendered to George Washington on October 19, 1781.

Although many consider the surrender at Yorktown as the end of the war, sporadic fighting continued in the South. Washington sent General Anthony Wayne to Georgia to

General Anthony Wayne was one of the military leaders George Washington relied on during the Revolutionary War. *(Library of Congress, Prints and Photographs Division [LC-USZ62-5667])*

The War for Independence

drive out the remaining British troops. In June 1782, General Wayne fought the last battle of the Revolution in Georgia when he defeated a few hundred American Indians who were allies of the British. By the end of July 1782, all the British troops and a number of the remaining Loyalists had left Savannah. By the end of the year, they were also gone from Charleston, and the thirteen American states had defeated the strongest military power of the time. Although the war was over, there was still much left to be done if the thirteen separate states with their vastly different histories were going to become one nation.

8

Building a Nation

When the British sailed away from Savannah in 1782, they left behind a state that had suffered much damage during the fighting between Patriots and Loyalists. Many of the plantations along the tidewater had belonged to Loyalists who had left. Many of the slaves who had worked the plantations had also disappeared. Large numbers of them had gone to Jamaica and other places in the Caribbean, where they formed their own communities. Others fled to Florida or to the frontier, where they lived among the Indians. Still others had been put to work by one side or the other in building fortifications during the war.

Prior to the war, the Georgia economy had been growing. Due to the fighting that took place in the later years of the war, agricultural export all but ceased. Because of the destruction of many plantations, the loss of slaves, and the loss of markets, the once profitable rice growing never rebounded after the war. Indigo, which had been the other cash crop of Georgia, was no longer marketable. The British had been the only market for American indigo. After the war, they refused to trade with their former colonies, and there was no other market for indigo.

Georgia, which had struggled to compete with the older and larger states, found itself in a tough spot after the Revolution. Over half the land that had been populated before the war had been abandoned. Food was scarce, and most people barely had enough

Once a profitable crop, indigo became worthless after the Revolutionary War because the British had been the only market for it. Its complicated manufacturing process is shown in this undated illustration. *(Library of Congress, Prints and Photographs Division [LC-USZ62-53584])*

to make it until harvest time in 1782. Georgia, like the 12 other states, also had substantial debts to pay after the war ended. Much of the debt was pay for those who had fought in and for Georgia.

In 1782, the state passed a law that they hoped would help them pay their debts. The Confiscation and Banishment Act of 1782 gave the state the authority to take and sell any land that had belonged to Loyalists. Although this generated some revenue and gave the state land, it was not enough. In 1784, the state passed a property tax to help fund the Georgia government.

One way that Georgia paid the debts it owed its soldiers was by granting them land. Anyone who had served in the Revolutionary War was granted 250 acres. The children of soldiers who had died in the war were granted 500 to 1,000 acres. Although this solved one problem, it created another. Georgia needed more land.

All the land that had been ceded to the colony and the state by the Creek was quickly being taken. The state government went about the task of making new treaties with the Creek. The major chiefs of the Creek were reluctant to give up any more land, and they avoided making new treaties. To get around this, the state negotiated land deals with lesser chiefs and small bands who may not have had the right to do so. However, any land that Georgia opened soon had settlers moving onto it. At this time, some settlers did not even wait for the government to gain title to the land. They illegally moved onto Indian land. These white settlers were considered squatters, and, along with the shady dealings of the state, they caused substantial friction along the Georgia frontier.

At the end of the Revolution in the Treaty of Paris, England had given Florida back to the Spanish. The Spanish officials were soon supplying guns and ammunition to the Creek as well as giving some of them a base to operate from if they wanted to raid Georgia settlements. Clashes between squatters and legal residents and the Creek became a frequent problem for the struggling state. Appeals to the federal government for help went unanswered for many reasons, and many in Georgia feared the possibility of a general uprising among the Creek.

THE ARTICLES OF CONFEDERATION

The Second Continental Congress had decided in 1776 that the government of the 13 united states needed to be formalized. A committee was formed in June 1776 to determine a plan for the federal government. The plan they came up with gave the federal government a great deal of power. When the plan was presented to

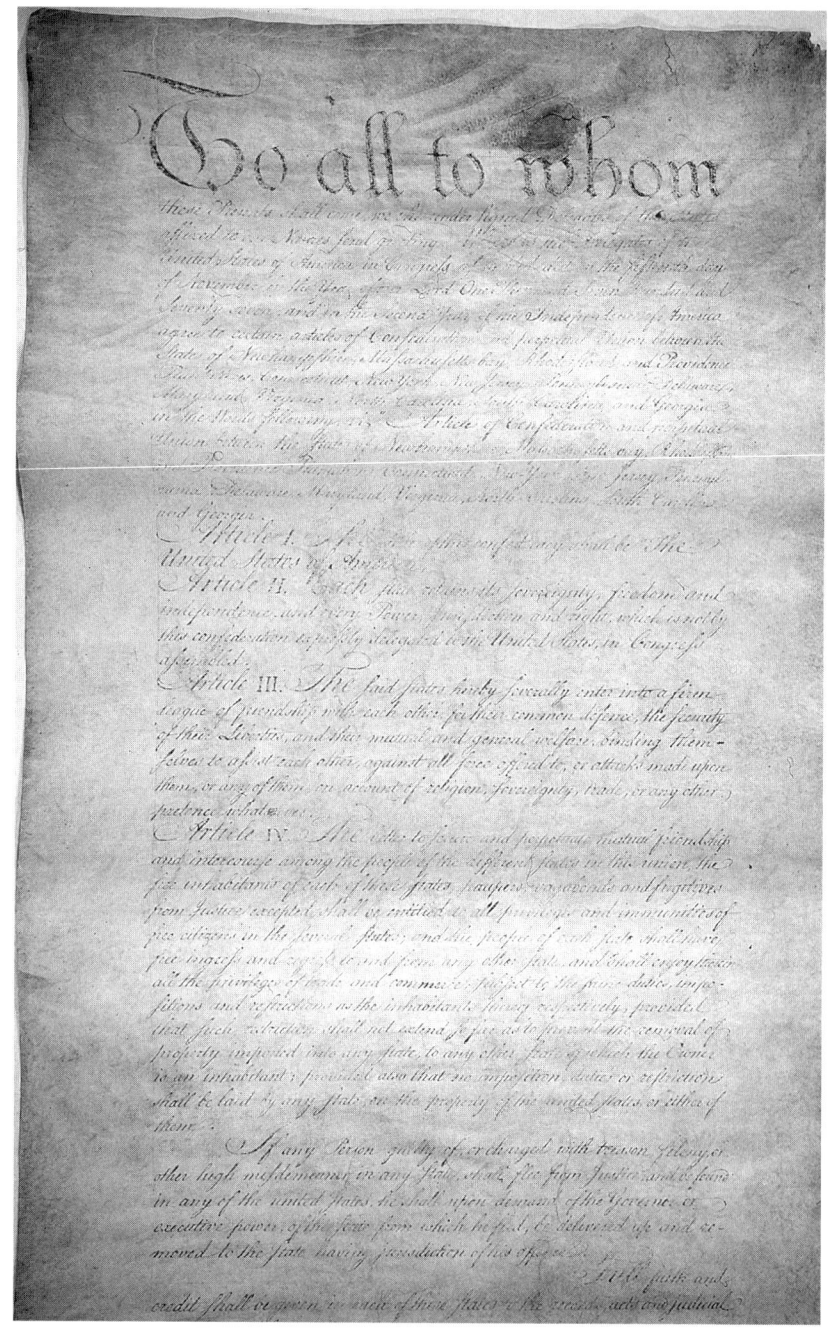

The Articles of Confederation, shown here, were written by a committee of the Continental Congress and intended as a constitution for the colonies.
(National Archives, National Archives Building [NWCTB-360-MISC-ROLL10F81])

the congress there were many objections. Many feared that a strong central government would merely replace the tyranny of the Crown. As debate continued over the proposal, many changes were made to limit the power of the federal government and ensure the sovereignty of the states.

In 1777, the congress approved a document known as the Articles of Confederation and sent it to the states to be ratified. Even this weak central government created problems for some. It was not ratified by all the states until 1781. As soon as the war ended, the shortcomings of the articles became even more apparent. The federal government had no say over the states and no way of raising taxes to support the government. Under the articles, the federal government was forced to ask the states for operating funds, and most of the time the states only gave a small portion of what was needed.

When farmers in western Massachusetts organized a tax revolt known as Shays's Rebellion, the state had to call out its own militia, as the federal army had been disbanded due to lack of funds. In Philadelphia, Pennsylvania, Revolutionary War veterans marched to the national capital to demand their as yet unpaid wages from the war. The congress could do nothing but run away. They left Philadelphia and moved the capital to Trenton, New Jersey.

For the people in Georgia, the lack of a strong federal government with the military ability to defend the states was a serious concern. The Creek and the Spanish were a real threat to the survival of the colony as it struggled to recover from the war. In 1786, a meeting was called for Annapolis, Maryland, that was intended to talk about a plan to help the states regulate trade and commerce. As it was, each state was able to make its own trade deals with foreign merchants, and the federal government had no ability to step in if the states ended up in disagreement.

Only five states, Delaware, New Jersey, New York, Pennsylvania, and Virginia sent delegates to Annapolis. There was little they could do, as any changes in the way the federal government functioned required all the states to agree. As the delegates talked, it became clear to them that something had to be done to strengthen the federal government's authority under the Articles of Confederation. At the urging of Alexander Hamilton, one of the delegates from New York, the Annapolis Convention sent a letter to the federal congress suggesting that a meeting be held in Philadelphia in 1787 to discuss amending the Articles of Confederation. Although the congress really did not have the authority to do so, it sent out a call to all the states to send delegates to a convention the following May.

THE CONSTITUTIONAL CONVENTION (1787)

Georgia was anxious to participate in the convention and selected Abraham Baldwin, William Few, William Houstoun, and William Pierce as its delegates to what soon turned into a constitutional convention. As the delegates started to debate changes to the Articles of Confederation in May 1787, they quickly decided that the articles were too flawed to save. They decided to write an entirely new constitution for the United States. Although scholars have questioned the authority of the convention to do what it did, the delegates acted out of necessity. Ultimately, they succeeded in creating the document under which the United States has operated for more than 200 years.

Creating the new constitution required serious debate, and many conflicting issues had to be resolved. Many in the North had already decided that the ideals of the Revolution were in opposition to slavery. This worried the delegates from the South, who saw slavery as a necessary evil for the economic success of their plantation economies. Because of the concern over slavery, the small southern states of Georgia and North and South Carolina formed an alliance with the delegates from the three largest states—Massachusetts, Pennsylvania, and Virginia. The three smaller states agreed to support some of the "big states" issues in

William Few represented Georgia at the Constitutional Convention and later served as U.S. senator. *(National Archives, Records of Exposition, Anniversary, and Memorial Commissions 148-CP-157)*

exchange for there being nothing in the Constitution that would affect slavery.

As the convention continued, the greatest stumbling block was the debate over representation in the federal legislature. The large states wanted to have representation proportional to population, giving them control in congress. A number of the smaller states wanted representation to be equal for every state no matter what its population. At first, Georgia and North and South Carolina went along with their alliance with the big states and supported proportional representation. Some of the smaller states threatened to walk out of the convention.

When a vote on representation was taken during the convention, there were only two of the Georgia delegates on the floor. Eleven of the 12 state delegations at the convention (Rhode Island did not send delegates) were present to vote on proportional representation. Five states voted for proportional representation and five voted against. One of the Georgia delegates voted with the alliance states. However, the other, Abraham Baldwin, believed that the small states were serious and would abandon the convention if they lost the vote, so he voted against the measure, ending the vote in a tie.

During the Constitutional Convention, Abraham Baldwin voted against proportional representation, a vote that ended in a tie and prompted the development of the Great Compromise. Baldwin represented Georgia for 18 years in the U.S. Congress. *(National Portrait Gallery, Smithsonian Institution)*

Because of Baldwin's vote, the plan for representation was sent back to a committee. In the committee, what is known as the Great Compromise was agreed upon. This plan called for a legislature made up of two houses. The Senate would have two senators from each state, which satisfied the small states. The House of Representatives would be based on population, with the larger states getting a proportionally greater number of representatives. This gave the large states a place where they would have a greater voice.

The Great Compromise created a legislative branch that has worked well with little change for more than 200 years. The number of representatives in the House of Representatives is

> **Preamble to the U.S. Constitution**
>
> *We the People of the United States, in Order to form a more perfect Union, establish Justice, insure domestic Tranquility, provide for the common defence, promote the general Welfare, and secure the Blessings of Liberty to ourselves and our Posterity, do ordain and establish this Constitution for the United States of America.*

adjusted every 10 years after the federal census is conducted. The idea of the census created another problem for the convention. How would slaves be counted in the census? The southern states wanted them counted, whereas the northern states felt they should only be counted if they were free. The delegates again had to come up with a compromise, and it can be found in Article 1, Section 2, of the Constitution. There it states that all "free persons" will be counted while only "three-fifths of all other Persons (slaves)" will count. This section also excludes untaxed Indians from the census.

The new constitution was approved by the convention on September 17, 1787. Abraham Baldwin and William Few signed the U.S. Constitution along with the delegates from the 11 other states. However, the rules that the convention had agreed to required nine of the states to ratify the Constitution before it would become the law of the land.

THE FOURTH STATE

For some states the process of ratifying the U.S. Constitution was long and drawn out. The people of Rhode Island were the last to ratify, and it took them until May 29, 1790. On June 21, 1788, New Hampshire was the ninth state to ratify, and the Constitution went into effect on that date. With their concerns about the Spanish and the Creek, Georgia was quick to ratify the Constitution. A state convention was held on January 2, 1788, and 24 delegates from across the state voted unanimously to ratify the Constitution, making it the fourth state to do so.

The Second Continental Congress convened on May 10, 1775, and remained in session until the newly independent nation had a constitution. *(National Archives, Still Picture Records [NWDNS-148-CCD-35])*

As Georgia took its place as one of the united states, it moved forward to provide public education for the people of the state. It also continued to guarantee religious freedom. The Anglican Church had lost its status as the only church supported by the colony, and it lost much of its power as many of its parishioners had been Loyalists. As the 18th century came to a close, the invention of the cotton gin by Eli Whitney would change the face of Georgia. Cotton would soon help Georgia to recover and then exceed the prosperity that had existed before the Revolution. As the last of the thirteen colonies to be established, Georgia played an important role in the creation of the United States, and it continues today to be the economic center of the South.

Georgia Time Line

1540
★ Hernando de Soto, with 600 Spanish soldiers, explores Georgia.

1566
★ A mission and fort are established by Pedro Menéndez de Avilés on Saint Catherine's Island off the Georgia coast.

1597
★ A Guale man, Juanillo, kills a priest who had tried to prevent him from becoming chief (*micco*).

1686
★ The Spanish abandon the Georgia coast.

1732
★ James Edward Oglethorpe and others, called trustees, are granted a charter for the colony of Georgia by George II.

1733
★ Oglethorpe sails up the Savannah River, landing at Yamacraw Bluff.

1739

★ The War of Jenkins' Ear between the British and the Spanish is fought with skirmishes on Georgia's southern border.

1742

★ The Battle of Bloody Marsh is fought near Fort Frederica.

1752

★ The trustees surrender their charter to the Crown, and Georgia becomes a royal colony.

1765

★ The Stamp Act is passed by Parliament; Georgia Governor James Wright is able to enforce the tax, unlike the other 12 colonies.

1774

★ Georgia is the only colony that does not send delegates to the First Continental Congress.

1775

★ After the battles at Lexington and Concord, Georgians take control of the government, choosing delegates for the Second Continental Congress.

1776

★ Georgians Lyman Hall, George Walton, and Button Gwinnett sign the Declaration of Independence.

1778

★ Savannah is captured by the British.

1782

★ Savannah is liberated, and the British troops evacuate the town.

1788

★ **January 2:** Georgia becomes the fourth state to ratify the U.S. Constitution.

Georgia Historical Sites

Augusta

Ezekiel Harris House   Tobacco merchant Ezekiel Harris built this house ca. 1797.

Address: 1840 Broad Street, Augusta, GA 30904
Phone: 706-724-0436
Web Site: www.inusa.com/tour/ga/augusta/harris.htm

Blakely

Kolomoki Mounds Historic Park   There are seven earthen mounds at Kolomoki Mounds Historic Park, built between A.D. 25 and 950.

Address: 205 Indian Mounds Road, Blakely, GA 39823
Phone: 800-864-7275
Web Site: www.gastateparks.org/info/kolomoki

Cartersville

Etowah Indian Mounds Historic Site   The Etowah Indian Mounds Historic Site has six mounds and other sites which were used between A.D. 1000 to A.D. 1550.

Address: 813 Indian Mounds Road SW, Cartersville, GA 30120
Phone: 770-387-3747
Web Site: www.gastateparks.org/info/etowah

Darien

Fort King Georgia Historic Site   Fort King George was used as the southernmost English outpost from 1721 to 1736. It eventually became the town Darien. It had been reconstructed and is open to the public.

Address: P.O. Box 711, Darien, GA 31305
Phone: 912-437-4770
Web Site: www.gastateparks.org/info/ftkinggeorge

Eatonton

Rock Eagle Effigy Mound   The Rock Eagle Effigy Mound, which is 120 feet wide and 102 feet long, was made by Mound Builders probably between 1000 B.C. and A.D. 1000.

Address: 350 Rock Eagle Road, Eatonton, GA 31024
Phone: 706-484-2862
Web Site: www.roadsidegeorgia.com/site/rock_eagle.html

Macon

Ocmulgee   The Ocmulgee National Monument Center commemorates 12,000 years of human habitation—from Ice Age hunters to the Mississippians, farming people who lived on the site for thousands of years.

Address: 1207 Emery Highway, Macon, GA 31217
Phone: 478-752-8257
Web Site: www.nps.gov/ocmu

MIDWAY

Fort Morris Historic Site Although initially victorious at Fort Morris, the Patriots were later defeated by the British on January 9, 1779.

Address: 2559 Fort Morris Road, Midway, GA 31320
Phone: 912-884-5999
Web Site: www.gastateparks.org/info/ftmorris

RINCON

Georgia Salzburger Society Museum Exhibits show the history of the early Salzburger and German settlers in Georgia.

Address: 2980 Ebenezer Road, Rincon, GA 31326
Phone: 912-754-7001
Web Site: www.museumsusa.org/data/museums/GA/134457.htm

SAVANNAH

Wormsloe Historic Site One of the earliest English settlers, Noble Jones built Wormsloe on the Isle of Hope. The ruins of the house are open to the public.

Address: 7601 Skidaway Road, Savannah, GA 31406
Phone: 912-353-3023
Web Site: www.gastateparks.org/info/wormsloe

WASHINGTON

Kettle Creek Battlefield On February 14, 1779, the Patriots defeated the British at the Battle of Kettle Creek, the only American victory in Georgia during the Revolution.

Address: Off Highway 44, 8 miles south of Washington, GA
Web Site: www.roadsidegeorgia.com/site/kettlecreek.html

Robert Toombs House Begun in 1797, this house was later the home of Robert Toombs, a planter and lawyer during the Civil War.

Address: 216 Robert Toombs Avenue, Washington, GA 30673
Phone: 706-678-2226
Web Site: www.gastateparks.org/info/rtoombs

Further Reading

Books

Britton, Tamara L. *The Georgia Colony*. Edina, Minn.: ABDO, 2001.

Coleman, Kenneth. *Colonial Georgia: a History*. New York: Scribner, 1976.

Fradin, Dennis Brindell. *The Georgia Colony*. Chicago: Children's Press, 1990.

Girod, Christina M. *Georgia*. San Diego, Calif.: Lucent, 2002.

Lommel, Cookie. *James Oglethorpe: Humanitarian and Soldier*. Philadelphia, Pa.: Chelsea House, 2001.

Web Sites

Golden Ink. "American Revolution in Georgia." Available online. URL: http://www.ngeorgia.com/history/nghistar.html. Downloaded on February 8, 2005.

———. "North Georgia History." Available online. URL: http://www.ngeorgia.com/history. Downloaded on February 8, 2005.

University of Georgia. Carl Vinson Institute of Government. "Georgia Info." Available online. URL: http://www.cviog.uga.edu/Projects/gainfo/gahist.htm. Downloaded on February 8, 2005.

———. Carl Vinson Institute of Government. "James Edward Oglethorpe Tercentenary Home Page." Available online. URL: http://www.cviog.uga.edu/Projects/jeo300. Downloaded on February 8, 2005.

Index

Page numbers in *italic* indicate photographs. Page numbers in **boldface** indicate box features. Page numbers followed by m indicate maps. Page numbers followed by c indicate time line entries. Page numbers followed by t indicate tables or graphs.

A

adventurers 35, 47, 64
Africa xv, **43, 52**
African Americans. *See* slavery and slaves
Africans 47, **56**
agriculture. *See* farming and farmers
alcohol 47, 54, 63, 75
Algonquian Indians 9
ambush 61
American Revolution 87–98. *See also* Declaration of Independence; independence movement
    aftermath of 99–101
    Battle of Brandywine 92
    Battle of Bunker Hill 89
    Battle of Lexington and Concord 86–89, 110c
    Georgia's role in the 89–90, 92, 94–95, 97–98
    Loyalists *vs.* Patriots in **73**. *See also* Loyalists; Patriots
    surrender of Lord Cornwallis 97
    war debt from 100–101
    and the war in Georgia 94–95, 97–98
    Battle of Yorktown 97
ammunition 101
Anglican Church 108. *See also* Church of England
Angus, George 79
Ann (ship) 36, 37, **90**
Annapolis, Maryland 83, 84, **84**
Annapolis Convention 103, 104
antlers (deer) 14
archbishop of Salzburg 49
army, Continental. *See* Continental army
arrows 14
Article 1, Section 2 (of U.S. Constitution) 106
Articles of Confederation 101, 102, 103, 104
artisans 34–35, 53
arts xiii
Ashley River 37
assistants 63
Athore (Timucuan chief) 18
Atlanta, Georgia 69
Augusta, Georgia 53, 69
Austenaco 6
Austria 49

B

Baldwin, Abraham 104–106, *105*
ball (deerskin) **11**
Barré, Isaac **76**
beans 7
bears 14
"Beloved Men" 9
benches (earthen) 10
Beaufort, South Carolina 37
Blackbeard 19
blockhouses 40, 41
blocks (of land) **40,** 41
Bloody Marsh, Battle of 61, 110c
blowguns 14
bones (deer) 14
Bosomworth, Mary Musgrove Matthews 38, 65, **65,** 66
Bosomworth, Thomas 65, **65,** 66
Boston, Massachusetts 80, 81, **84**
Boston Massacre 80, 81, *81*
Boston Port Bill 83
Boston Tea Party **76,** 82, *82*, 83

117

bows 14
boycott (of British goods) 80, 85
Brandywine, Battle of 92
Bray, Thomas 32–33
Britain. *See* England; Great Britain
British East India Company 82
British Empire (in North America) 44m
British forces
    Battle of Lexington and Concord 86–89
    Battle of Yorktown 97
    Boston Massacre 80, 81, 81
    capture Philadelphia 92
    in Georgia 94, 95, 97, 98, 110c, 111c
    in the North 90, 92
    and plan to capture the South 94
    and Savannah 97, 110c, 111c
"brother to war" **11**
buffalo 14
buildings
    ceremonial lodges 9
    city planning **40**
    housing 9, 10, 40, **40,** 41, 53, 56, 57, 96
    mud and wattle 9, 10
    public 13
Bull, William 40, **40,** 41
Bulloch, Archibald 90, **90**
Bunker Hill, Battle of 89

C

Cabot, John 1, 2
Cahokia xvii, 7, 8
Calvin, John xiv
Calvinistic Methodists **50**
Campbell, Lord William 92
Canada xiii
cannibalism 18
cannons 40, 41, 89
Caribbean
    Dutch settlement in xvi
    slaves in 14, 99
    and Spain xv, 2, **20**
    sugar from 74, 75
Carolana 2
    expedition to 18
    and Spain 16, 20, **20**
    treasure ships near 17

Caroline, Fort 20
cash crops **35,** 99
Castell, Robert 31, 32
Castillo de San Marcos 27, 60
Catalina 23
Catholic Church xiii, xvii
Catholicism and Catholics
    banning of 71
    in colony of Georgia 34
    in France 16, **16,** 18, 71
    in Maryland 47
    and missions 21–24, 22–25, 27, 28, 109c
    priests 21–23, 109c
    and Protestants 47
cattle 37, 94
Census, U.S. 106
Central America xvii, 2
ceremonies 12–13
charity colonists 34, 35
    and land restrictions 47
    success of 53
    support for 50
Charles I (king of England) 2
Charles I (king of Spain and [as Charles V] Holy Roman Emperor) 2
Charles II (king of England) 25, 25
Charlesfort 17, 20
Charles River 37
Charleston, South Carolina 25, 26m
    capture of 97
    freeing of 98
    liberty pole in **84**
Charles Town 25, 26m, 37, 37m
charter(s)
    for colony of Georgia 33, 37, 62, 109c
    English xvi
    Massachusetts 83
Cherokee Indians 4
    Austenaco 6
    Iroquoian language family 6
    map of, in Georgia 5m
    resettlement of 15
    trade with 25
Chiaha Indians 4, 5m
China **35**
Choctaw Indians 11

Christianity and Christians 34, 47. *See also specific headings, e.g.:* Catholicism and Catholics
chunkey **11**
churches **40**
Church of England 47, 71. *See also* Anglican Church
circular letter **77,** 80
city planning **40, 40**
climate **43**
Coercive Acts 83. *See also* Intolerable Acts of 1774
Coligny, Gaspard de 16, 18
colonial assembly (election of) 64
colonists
    charity 34, 35, 47, 50, 53
    and disease 42, 43, **43**
    origin of 71
colonization. *See also* settlements
    and disease 41, 42, **43**
    by England 2, 28–29, 36–38
    by France 14, 16–18, 20
    by René Goulaine de Laudonnière 18, 18, 20
    and Margravate of Azilia **28**
    and religious persecution 47
    by Jean Ribault 18
    and slavery 53
    by Spain xv, 2, 14, 16, 17, 20
colony of Carolina 25
colony of Georgia 110c. *See also* Georgia; royal colony; *specific headings, e.g.:* Savannah, Georgia
    attack on 61
    and Catholics 34
    charter for 33, 37, 62, 109c
    defense of 41, 47, 59
    early settlement in 47–53
    Benjamin Franklin 80
    and French and Indian wars **68**
    growth of 46, 47, **68**
    joins the American Revolution 89–90, 92, 94
    life in 46–62
    maps of 36m, 58m
    James Edward Oglethorpe. *See* Oglethorpe, James Edward
    and Salzburgers 50–51
    and Spain 53, 58–61, 109c

and the Stamp Act Congress **77**
trustees of. *See* trustees
War of Jenkins' Ear 58, 59, 110c
Columbus, Christopher xiii, xv, xv, 1, **8,** 25
Columbus, Georgia 69
commerce 103. *See also* merchants; trade
Commons House 66, 67, 89
companies xvi, 82
Concord, Massachusetts. *See* Lexington and Concord, Battle of
Confiscation and Banishment Act of 1782 101
Congress, U.S. *See* U.S. Congress
Connecticut xviii*m*
constitution (of Georgia) **91**
Constitution, U.S. *See* U.S. Constitution
Constitutional Convention (1787) 104–106
Continental army. *See also* militia; Patriots
   at Battle of Brandywine 92
   and George Washington 90
   in Georgia 94, 95, 95, 97
Continental Congress 102, 107
Continental Congress, First 84–86, 85, 89, 110c
Continental Congress, Second 85, 86
   Declaration of Independence 93
   Georgia's delegates to the 90, **90, 91,** 110c
conversion (religious)
   of Native Americans 21–25, 47
   of John Wesley 48
Cooke, William 61, 62
cooking fires 13
corn 7, **8,** 9, 12–13
Cornwallis, Lord 97
Corpa, Father Pedro 23
cotton 54, 108
county 63
courts 66
Cox, Dr. William 35, 37, 43
Creek Indians 4, 27
   alliance with English of 14–15
   armed by Spain 101
   and Mary Bosomworth 38, 65, **65,** 66
   games of the **11,** 12

Green Corn Festival 12–13
land from 69, 70*m*, 101
life of 9–15
map of, in Georgia 5*m*
and Mound Builders 6
resettlement of 15
subgroups of 8
as threat to state of Georgia 103, 106
trade with 25
Treaty of Augusta 69, 70*m*
villages of the 9, 10, 12
and Yamacraw 38
Creek War 15
crops
   cash **35**
   corn 7, **8,** 9, 12–13
   cotton 54, 108
   grown by Native Americans 7, **8**
   indigo **35,** 69, 99, 100
   rice **35,** 37, 57, 69, 92, 93, 99
   silk 33, **35,** 69
   tobacco 7, 12, 13, **35**
Cumberland Island 22, 23, 23
customshouse 80, 81

D

Darien, Georgia 24, 52
Dark Ages (Middle Ages) xiii
deaths 41, 42, **55, 56**
debt
   from American Revolution 100–101
   Parliament and 68–69, 71, 73, 75
debtors 32, 34, **34**
Declaration of Independence **92,** 93
   Button Gwinnett 91, **92,** 110c
   Lyman Hall 90, **90,** 90, 110c
   support for **91–92**
   George Walton 91, **92,** 110c
Declaratory Act 79
deer 13, 14
deerskin 14
defense
   under Articles of Confederation 103
   of colony of Georgia 41, 47, 59
   communities for 53
Delaware xviii*m*, 47

Delaware River 92
Dempsey, Charles 59
dent corn **8**
dice 76
direct tax 79, 80
disease
   and colonists 41, 42, **43**
   dysentery 43, **56**
   and mosquitoes 41
   and Native Americans 2, 4, 8
   and slavery 36, **43, 56**
   smallpox 4, 8, 32
documents (legal) 75
Dooly, John **96**
drinking
   excessive 47
   water 43
the Dutch xv–xvi, 29
dye 69
dysentery 43, **56**

E

eagle (earthen) 6–7, 7
ear (of Robert Jenkins) **59**
earthen mounds xvii, 6–7, 14
Eatonton, Georgia 7
Ebenezer 51, 51
economy
   after the American Revolution 99, 100
   and cotton 108
   plantation 47, 57, 104
education, public 108
effigies, burning of 79
Egypt **55**
election (of colonial assembly) 64
Ellis, Henry **65,** 68
England. *See also* British forces; Parliament
   alliance with Creek Indians of 14–15
   anti-Catholic feelings in 71
   attack on St. Augustine by 27, 28
   John Cabot 1, 2
   Charles I 2
   Charles II 25, 25
   colonization by 2, 28–29, 36–38
   French and Indian wars 57, **68,** 71, 73

England (continued)
- George II (king of Great Britain) 33, **33**
- King George's War 57
- land claims of 2, 25, 59
- London **40**
- map of British Empire in North America 44m
- James Edward Oglethorpe 36–38, 61–62
- religious persecution in 47
- return of Florida by 101
- and Jean Ribault 18
- and Salzburgers 49
- settlement by xvi, xvii
- and Spain xv, **20**, 25, 27–30, 57, 58
- stamp tax in 76
- War of Jenkins' Ear 57–62, **59**, 94, 110c
- Dr. Henry Woodward **26**

equal representation 105
Estaing, Jean-Baptiste-Charles-Henri-Hector d' 95, 97
Etowah Indian mounds 6, 112–113
Europe xiii–xiv, xvii. *See also specific headings, e.g.:* England
executive branch (weak) **91**
exploration
- Africa xv
- John Cabot 1, 2
- Christopher Columbus xiii, xv, xv, 1, **8**, 25
- by France 17
- Hernando de Soto 2–4, 3m, 4, 6, 8, 109c
- Giovanni da Verrazano 2, 16
- Vikings xiii, xiv

Ezekiel Harris House 112

F

fall line 69
Far East xv
farming and farmers. *See also* crops; plantations
- and burning of farms 94
- changes in practices of 69
- and corn 7, **8**, 9, 12–13
- and defensive communities 53
- land for 40
- and Native Americans 7, **8**, 9, 13, 14
- revolt of 103
- smaller size farms 71
- and women 14

federal government 101, 103
Few, William 104, 104, 106
First Continental Congress. *See* Continental Congress, First
fishing 14
fleet 61, 97. *See also* shipping and ships
Fleet Prison, London 31, 32
Florida xv
- during American Revolution 94
- attacked by Oglethorpe 60, 60–61
- Fort Caroline 20
- Robert Jenkins and **59**
- returned to Spain 101
- St. Augustine. *See* St. Augustine, Florida
- Saint Mary's River 27
- slaves in 99
- and Spain 14, 16, 22, 28, 59, 101
- Tampa Bay 3
- threat from 103

Florida Rangers 94
flour corn **8**
food 53
foraging 14
Fort Caroline 20
Fort Frederica. *See* Frederica, Fort
Fort King Georgia Historic Site 113
Fort Morris Historic Site 114
forts 47, 53
Fort St. Simon. *See* St. Simon, Fort
Fort Sunbury 94
France
- and American Revolution 92, 95, 97
- and Catholicism 16, **16**, 18, 71
- colonization by 14, 16–18, 20
- French and Indian wars 57, **68**, 71, 73
- Huguenots 16, **16**, 29
- land claims of 2, 16
- Jean Ribault 16–18, 18, 20
- and Spain 20, **20**, 21

Giovanni da Verrazano 2, 16
War of Jenkins' Ear 57–62, **59**, 94, 110c
Franklin, Benjamin 79, 80
Frederica, Fort
- Battle of Bloody Marsh 110c
- county centered at 63
- founding of 53
- map of 58m, 64m
- retreat to 61

Frederick, Lord North 83
freedom of religion. *See* religious freedom
French and Indian Wars 57, **68**, 71, 73
French civil war 18

G

Gage, General 89
galleons xvi
games 11, **11**, 12
George II (king of Great Britain) 33, 33
Georgia xviiim. *See also* colony of Georgia; *specific headings, e.g.:* Savannah, Georgia
- aftermath of American Revolution in 99–101
- and anti-British sentiment 72, 73
- birth date of 39
- at Constitutional Convention 104, 105
- declares independence **91–92**
- first exploration of 4
- ratifies U.S. Constitution 106, 111c
- threat by Spain to 103, 106
- war debt of 100–101
- the war in 94–95, 97–98

Georgia, colony of. *See* colony of Georgia
Georgia Assembly 64
The Georgia Gazette 78, 79, 83
Georgia Salzburger Society Museum 114
glass 80
gold 17, **19**
Golden Hill, Battle of 80
Gosnold, Bartholomew xvi

government
   county 63
   federal 101, 103
   royal 66–71
   state **91**
governor(s)
   Henry Ellis **65,** 68
   Robert Johnson 37, 40
   John Reynolds 66, 67, 67
   James Wright 72, 72, 73, 79, 83, 84, 90, 95, 110c
granaries 9, 10, 14
grape vines 33
Great Awakening 48
Great Britain. *See also* England
   anti-Catholic feelings in 71
   French and Indian wars 57, **68**
   King George's War 57
Great Compromise 105
Green Corn Festival 12–13
Grenville, George 75
Guale (Indian leader) 21
Guale region 21–24, 109c
Gulf of Mexico 3
gunpowder 89
guns 101
Gwinnett, Button 91, **92,** 110c

H

Hall, Lyman 90, **90,** 90, 110c
Hamilton, Alexander 104
Hancock, John 80
Hart, Benjamin **96**
Hart, Nancy 96, **96**
harvest season 14
Herbert, Henry 35–37
hides (deer) 14
Hispaniola 2
Hitchiti Indians 4, 5m
Hollywood Indian mounds 6
"Holy Club" **50**
Holy Roman Empire 49
hooves (deer) 14
House of Representatives. *See* U.S. House of Representatives
housing
   beach house 53
   blockhouses 40, 41
   cabin of Nancy Hart 96
   city planning **40**
   for colonists 40
   for slaves 56, 57
   summer and winter 9, 10
Houstoun, John 90, **90**
Houston, William 104
Huguenots 16, **16,** 18, 29
hunting 13, 13, 14
hymns **50**

I

illegal trade 73, 75
Illinois 7, 8
imports 80
indentured servants 52, **52**
independence movement 72–86. *See also* Declaration of Independence
   First Continental Congress 84–86, 85, 89, 110c
   Second Continental Congress 85, 86, 90, **90,** **91,** 93, 110c
   Georgia declares independence **91–92**
   Intolerable Acts 83–85
   Loyalists vs. Patriots in **73**. *See also* Loyalists; Patriots
   Stamp Act 75–77, **76,** 77, **77,** 78, 79, 110c
   the Stamp Act Congress 77
   Sugar Act 75
   Tea Act **76,** 82, 83
   Townshend Duties 79–81
Indian Territory 15
indigo **35,** 69, 99, 100
indirect tax 80
insects 42
Intolerable Acts of 1774 83–85
Ireland 2, 25, 71
Iroquoian language family 6

J

Jackson, Andrew 15
Jamaica 99
Jefferson, Thomas **84, 92**
Jenkins, Robert 59
Jenkins' Ear **59**
Jews 43, 44, 71
Johnson, Robert 37, 40
Jones, Noble W. 90, **90**
Joseph's Town 52
Juanillo 23, 24, 109c

K

Kettle Creek Battlefield 114
King George's War 57, **68**
King Georgia Historic Site, Fort 113
King William's War 68
Kolomoki Indian mounds 6, 112

L

lacrosse **11,** 11
land
   allotment of 40
   for colonists 35, 57
   confiscation of 101
   from Creek Indians 69, 70m, 101
   and Native Americans xvii
   need for more 101
   ownership 64, 66, 67, 69–71
   restrictions on 47
   and social divisions 69–71
land claims
   and Mary Bosomworth 65, **65,** 66
   of England 2, 25, 59
   of France 2, 16
   of Spain 1, 2, 3m, 59
land grants 25, 66
"land of Charles" 2
Laudonnière, René Goulaine de 18, 18, 20
law making 66
lead 80
legislature
   representation in 105–106
   under royal government 66, 67
Lexington and Concord, Battle of 86–89, 110c
Liberty (ship) 80
"Liberty Boys" **76**
liberty poles and trees 83, 84, **84**
licenses 76
Lincoln, Benjamin 95, 95
lodges (ceremonial) 9
London, England **40**
lots, city **40**
Louisiana 14, 28, **68**
Lower Creek Indians 8
Loyalists
   after the war 99, 101
   and Anglican Church 108

Loyalists (continued)
    fighting in Savannah of 92–93
    in Florida 94
    in Georgia 73, 89, 92–93, 95, 96, 97–99
    and Nancy Hart 96
    high percentage of 73
    Patriots vs. 73
    petitions of 83, 84
    in the South 92
loyalty oaths 95
Luther, Martin xiv
Lutheran Church 49

M

Macon, Georgia 69
Maine xviiim
malaria 43
malnutrition 36
Manhattan xvi
Margravate of Azilia 28
market, slave 55
Maryland xviiim
    cash crops in 35
    and English Catholics 47
    and slavery 55
Massachusetts xviiim
    anti-British sentiment in 72
    Battle of Bunker Hill 89
    Battle of Lexington and Concord 86–89, 110c
    Boston 80, 81, **84**
    Boston Massacre 80, 81, 81
    Boston Tea Party **76,** 82, 82, 83
    circular letter from **77,** 80
    at Constitutional Convention 104
    Shays's Rebellion 103
    ties to England of 73
Massachusetts Government Act 83
Mathew (ship) 1
McIntosh, John 94
melons 13
men, Native American 13, 14
Méndez de Canzo, Gonzalo 23, 24
Menéndez de Avilés, Pedro 20–22, 109c
merchants
    and illegal trade 73, 75
    and Jenkin's Ear 59
    and Sugar Act 75
    and trade with Spain 57, 58
Methodism
    Charles Wesley 47, 48, 49, **50**
    John Wesley 47–48, 48, **50**
    George Whitefield 47, 48, **50,** 50
micco 9, 38, 109c
Middle Ages xiii
middle passage **55, 56**
militia. *See also* Continental army; Patriots
    capture of 95
    Battle of Lexington and Concord 86–89
    in War of Jenkins' Ear 60, 61
missionaries
    revolt against 23–24
    Charles Wesley 47, 48, 49, **50**
    John Wesley 47–48, 48, **50**
missions (Spanish) 21–24, 22–25, 27, 28, 109c
Mississippi River Valley 4, 6
molasses 75
Montgomery, Sir Robert **28,** 29
Moore, James 27, 28
Moravians 47–48, 52, 53
Morris Historic Site, Fort 114
mosquitoes 41, **43**
Mound Builders 6
    abandonment of sites of 8
    Cahokia xvii, 7, 8
    crops of 13
    Etowah Indian mounds 6, 112–113
    Rock Eagle Mound 6–7, 7, 113
mud (as building material) 9, 10
mulberry trees 33, **35,** 69
Musgrove, John 38, **65**
Musgrove, Mary 38. *See also* Bosomworth, Mary Musgrove Matthews
Muskogean language 6
Muskogee Indians 6. *See also* Creek Indians
mutiny 17

N

Native Americans 4–15. *See also specific headings, e.g.:* Creek Indians
    allied with British 98
    Athore 18
    attack on missions by 23–25, 27
    Austenaco 6
    Mary Bosomworth 38, 65, **65,** 66
    Cherokee Indians 4, 5m, 6, 6, 15, 25
    colonists disguised as 82, 82
    conversion of 21–25, 47
    and corn 7, **8,** 9, 12–13
    counted for representation 106
    and deer 13, 14
    and disease 2, 4, 8
    farming by 7, **8,** 9, 13, 14
    and French and Indian wars **68**
    and hunting 13, 13, 14
    lacrosse **11,** 11
    and land xvii, 69, 70m, 101
    and James Edward Oglethorpe 38, 38
    palisades 10, 10
    population of xvii
    and slavery 2, 14, 24
    and Hernando de Soto 4, 6, 8
    tobacco 13
    trade with 14, 17, 25, 63
    and trustees 38
    villages of 9, 10, 12
    in War of Jenkins' Ear 60–61
    women 14
    and Dr. Henry Woodward 26
    Yamacraw Indians 38, 38, 39, 58m
    Yamasee Indians 4, 5m, 14, 28
naval ships 61, 97
New Ebenezer 52
New England 47, 48, 75
Newfoundland xiii
New Hampshire xviiim, **77,** 106
New Jersey xviiim, **76,** 92
newspaper 78, 79
New World xv
New York City 80, 83, 94
New York State xvi, xviiim, **92**
nobility 52
North, the 87–90, 92, 104
North America
    English settlement xvi, xvii
    land claims in 2
    map of British Empire in 44m
    Spanish exploration of 2–4

North Bridge 89
North Carolina xviiim
    cash crops in **35**
    at Constitutional Convention 104, 105
    Spanish settlement in 16
    and the Stamp Act Congress **77**
"no taxation without representation" 76
Nova Scotia xiii
Nunis, Dr. Samuel 43

O

oaths of loyalty 95
occupation of Georgia 97
Ocmulgee 6, 113
Ogeechee River 52
Oglethorpe, James Edward 30, 31, 32, **34**
    arrival in Georgia of 36–38
    attacks on Florida by 60, 60–61
    beach house of 53
    and Mary Bosomworth **65**
    control of rules by 47
    and defense of colony 41
    and the laying out of Savannah 39–41, **40**, 43
    lifting of rule of 54, 57
    and Native Americans 38, 38
    and plans to colonize Georgia 33–34
    and prison conditions 31–33, **34**
    returns to England 61–62
    and the Salzburgers 50–52
    security concerns of 59
    as trustee 35, 109c
    and War of Jenkins' Ear 94
Oglethorpe, Theophilus **34**
Okefenokee National Wildlife Refuge 42
Oklahoma 4, 15
Old North Church 87
olive trees 33
Ottoman Turks xv

P

palisades 10, 10, 40
paper, painter's 80

Parliament
    Declaratory Act 79
    Intolerable Acts 83
    and James Edward Oglethorpe 31, **34**, 59, 62
    Stamp Act 76, **77**, 110c
    Sugar Act 77
    support for charity colonists from 50
    Tea Act 82, 83
    Townshend Duties 79–81
    and war debt 68–69, 71, 73, 75
    War of Jenkins' Ear **59**
Patriots. *See also* Sons of Liberty
    Battle of Lexington and Concord 86–89
    circular letter to **77**
    in Georgia 73, 89, 90, **90,** 92–93, 95, 97
    Loyalists *vs.* **73**
    in the North 90, 92
    petitions of 83
    in Savannah 89, 92–93
    Stamp Act 76
    Tondee's Tavern 83
    Townshend Duties 80, 81
peace treaty (with Creek Indians) 38
Pennsylvania xviiim
    at Constitutional Convention 104
    and Declaration of Independence **91**
    Benjamin Franklin 80
    and French and Indian wars **68**
    Quakers in 47
petitions **77,** 83, 84
Philadelphia, Pennsylvania
    capture of 92
    city planning **40**
    First Continental Congress 85, 85
    protest of soldiers in 103
pigs 37
pipes (of Native Americans) 13
pirates 19, **19, 20,** 21, 25
plantation economy 47, 57, 104
plantation(s)
    docks for 69
    French and Spanish 73, 75
    and indentured servants **52**

    and large landowners 70
    of the Loyalists 99
    and slavery 54, 56, 70
    in South Carolina 53, 54
playing cards 76
popcorn **8**
population
    in 1740–1790 46t
    after the war 99
    along Savannah River 69
    of Cahokia 8
    counting of, for representation 106
    growth of 46, 46t, 47
    of Native Americans xvii
    of slaves **56,** 57
Port Royal, South Carolina 37, 59
Port Royal Sound, South Carolina 17, 17m
potatoes, sweet 13
poverty **34,** 71
president, county 63
priests 21–23, 109c
prison(s)
    debtors 32, **34**
    Fleet Prison 31
    and James Edward Oglethorpe 31–33, **34**
    and Jean Ribault 18
privateers **19, 20,** 21, **26**
proportional representation 105, 106
proprietors of Carolina **28**
Protestant Reformation xiv
Protestants
    Calvinistic Methodists **50**
    and Catholics 47
    and civil war in France 18
    Huguenots 16, **16,** 18, 29
    Methodists 47–48, 48–50, **50**
    Moravians 47–48, 52, 53
    Salzburgers 49–52, 51
    settlement by xvi
    toleration of 71
protests. *See also* revolts
    of soldiers 103
    against Stamp Act 76, **76,** 77
    of Townshend Duties 80, 81
Provincial Congress 89–90, **91**
public education 108

Index 123

public square
    and city planning **40,** 41
    in Creek villages 10, 12, 13
    and Green Corn Festival 13
pumpkins 13
Puritans 47
Purry, Jean-Pierre 29–30, **35**
Purrysburgh 29, 29–30
pyramids 6

Q

Quakers 47
Queen Anne's War 27, **68**

R

raiding 94
ratification 103, 106, 108, 111c
rattles 14
Red Bluff 51
redcoats 87, 89. *See also* British forces
"red town" 9
religion
    Catholics. *See* Catholicism and Catholics
    and conversion 21–25, 47, 48
    Protestants. *See* Protestants
    Puritans 47
religious freedom (toleration)
    in colony of Georgia 33, 34
    and Huguenots **16**
    in Savannah 43
    and settlers 71
    in state of Georgia 108
religious persecution 47
Renaissance xiv
renting of slaves 54
representation
    and land ownership 64, 66, 67
    no taxation without 76
    proportional 105, 106
Revere, Paul 87, 88
revolts 23–24, 103. *See also* protests
Reynolds, John 66, 67, 67
Rhode Island xviiim, 105, 106
Ribault, Jean 16–18, 18, 20
rice **35,** 37, 92, 93
    after the war 99
    growing of 69
    plantations 57
rifles 96

Robert Toombs House 115
Rock Eagle Mound 6–7, 7, 113
Roman Empire xiii, **55**
royal charters. *See* charters
royal colony
    Henry Ellis **65,** 68
    Georgia as a 62–71, 110c
    rapid growth in 69
    John Reynolds 66, 67, 67
    James Wright 72, 72, 73, 79, 83, 84, 90, 95, 110c
rum
    ban on 54
    in New England 75
    James Edward Oglethorpe and 47

S

Saint Andrews Club 52
St. Augustine, Florida 20, 24, 25
    during American Revolution 94
    attack on 27, 27, 28, 60, 61
    and England 27, 27, 28, 59
    Dr. Henry Woodward in **26**
Saint Catherine's Island 20, 22, 25, 109c
St. John's College 84, **84**
St. Johns River 20
Saint Louis, Missouri 7
St. Mary's, Georgia 21
Saint Mary's River 27
St. Simon, Fort 59, 61
St. Simon's Island 53, 58m
Salzburgers 49–52, 51
Sanchez, Francisco de Moral 59
San Pedro 23
Savannah, Georgia 38
    attempt to recapture 95, 97
    capture of 95, 110c
    and city planning **40,** 41, 58m
    county centered at 63
    fighting in 92–93
    Intolerable Acts 83
    the laying out of 39–41, 43
    liberation of 98, 111c
    Moravians in 52
    Patriots in 89, 92–93
    Scots in 52
    soldiers to protect 94
    Sons of Liberty 76

Savannah River 29, 29, 58m
    Joseph's Town 52
    population along 69
    settlement near 28, 51, 52
    small farms near 71
    Yamacraw Bluff 37–38, 40, **40,** 109c
Scandinavians xiii
science xiii
Scotland and Scots 2, 25, 52, 71
scurvy **56**
Second Continental Congress. *See* Continental Congress, Second
Secotan, village of 9
self-government 63
Senate, U.S. *See* U.S. Senate
settlement(s). *See also* colonization
    control of by Oglethorpe 47
    Dutch xvi
    early 47–53
    English xvi, xvii, 14–15, 28, 73
    French 14
    Jewish 43, 44
    Moravian 52, 53
    Protestant xvi
    Salzburger 49–52
    Scottish 52
    Spanish 14, 16
Seven Year's War. *See* French and Indian wars
Shays's Rebellion 103
shellfish 14
shipping and ships
    English 18, **59**
    fighting over 92–93
    fleets 61, 97
    galleons xvi
    merchant **59**
    oceangoing 69
    outfitting of 36
    papers for 76
    of Jean Ribeault 20
    seizure of 58
    Spanish xvi, 17, **20,** 25
    and stamp acts 79
shooting competitions 41
Siege of Boston **84**
silk **35**
silkworms 33, **35,** 69
silver 17, **19**

sinew 14
slavery and slaves 53–54, **55, 56,** 57
    after the American Revolution 99
    and Constitutional Convention 104
    counted of, for representation 106
    and disease **43**
    in early Georgia 40
    housing for 56, 57
    and indentured servants **52**
    legalization of 56, 57
    market for 55
    and Native Americans 2, 14, 24
    opposition to 47
    picking cotton 54
    and plantations 70
    in population **56,** 57
    prohibition on 63, 64
smallpox 4, 8, 32
Smith John xvi
smuggling 75
social division 69–71
Society for Promoting Christian Knowledge 49
soldiers 61, 101, 103
Sons of Liberty **76**
    Boston Tea Party 82, 82, 83
    liberty poles 84, **84**
    Stamp Act 76, 79
    Townshend Duties 80
Soto, Hernando de 2–4, 4, 109c
    and disease 8
    and Native Americans 4, 6, 8
    route of 3m
South, the 94, 104
South America xvi, xvii, 2
South Carolina xviiim, 30
    cash crops in **35**
    concerns for security in 28
    at Constitutional Convention 104, 105
    and Declaration of Independence **91, 92**
    Robert Johnson 37, 40
    militia from 60
    and slavery 53, 54
    Sons of Liberty **76**
    Spanish settlement in 16

    support for Georgia colonists by 37–38
    troops from 97
    Dr. Henry Woodward **26**
Southeast Culture Area 5
Spain
    and Caribbean xv, 2, **20**
    and Carolana 16, 20, **20**
    as Catholic country 71
    Charles I 2
    colonization by xv, 2, 14, 16, 17, 20
    and colony of Georgia 53, 58–61, 109c
    Christopher Columbus xiii, xv, xv, 1, **8,** 25
    and Creek Indians 101
    and England xv, **20,** 25, 27–30, 57, 58
    and Florida 14, 16, 22, 28, 59, 101
    and France 20, **20,** 21
    King George's War 57
    land claims of 1, 2, 3m, 59
    missions of 21–24, 22–25, 27, 28, 109c
    plantations of 73, 75
    and shipping xvi, 17, **20,** 25
    Hernando de Soto 2–4, 3m, 4, 6, 8, 109c
    as threat to state of Georgia 103, 106
    trade with 57, 58
    treasure of 17, **19, 20,** 21
    War of Jenkins' Ear 110c
    Dr. Henry Woodward **26**
Spanish Armada xv, xvi
spears 14
Speedwell (ship) 79
squash 7, 13
squatters 101
The Stamp Act Congress 77
Stamp Act of 1765 75–77, 79, 110c
    colonists denouncing 77
    The Georgia Gazette 78
    Sons of Liberty **76**
    The Stamp Act Congress **77**
stamp agents 76, **77, 78**
stamps 76, 76, 79
states, sovereignty of 103

Sterling Bluff 52
stockades 10
sugar 73, 74, 75, 75
Sugar Act of 1764 75
sugar plantations 14
summers 41
Sunbury, Fort 94
swamps 42
sweet corn **8**
sweet potatoes 13
Switzerland 29, 30

T

Tamathli Indians 4, 5m
Tampa Bay, Florida 3
taxation 71
    and Articles of Confederation 103
    Intolerable Acts 83–85
    Stamp Act 75–77, 76, **76,** 77, **77,** 78, 79, 110c
    the Stamp Act Congress 77
    Sugar Act 75
    Tea Act **76,** 82, 83
    Townshend Duties 79–81
    and war debt 73
    without representation 76
tea 80–83
Tea Act of 1773 **76,** 82, 83
Teach, Edward 19
"tea parties" **76,** 83
The Thirteen Colonies, 1790 xviiim
Thunderbolt 53
tidewater (region) 69, 71, 99
Timucuan Indians 18
tobacco 7, 12, 13, **35**
Tomochichi (Yamacraw leader) 39
Tondee's Tavern 83, 89
tools (from deer) 14
Toonahowi 39
towns, Creek Indian 9
Townshend, Charles 80
Townshend Duties 79–81
trade. *See also* merchants
    in deer hides 14
    Far East xiii
    illegal 73, 75
    with Native Americans 14, 17, 25, 63
    restrictions on, with Georgia 89

Index

trade (continued)
  with Spain 57, 58
  states' regulation of 103
  of sugar 73, 74, 75, 75
tradesmen 34–35, 53
trading network 28
trading posts 30, 38, **65**
traps 14
treasure, Spanish 17, **19, 20,** 21
treaty (over land claims) 59
Treaty of Augusta 69, 70m
Treaty of Paris 101
tribes 4, 5m. *See also* Native Americans
troops 59, 94, 97
trustees (of colony of Georgia)
  and defense of colony 41
  final years of rule of the 63–64, 66
  grant of charter to 109c
  lifting of Oglethorpe's rules by 54, 57
  and Native Americans 38
  James Oglethorpe as 62, 109c. *See also* Oglethorpe, James Edward
  recruiting of colonists by 34–36, 53
  and royal charter 33
  and Salzburgers 50–51
  and silk 35
  surrender charter 110c
turkeys, wild 14

U

"unfortunate poor" 34
up-country 95, 97
Upper Creek Indians 8
U.S. Census 106
U.S. Congress 105–106
U.S. Constitution 107. *See also* Articles of Confederation
  Article 1, Section 2 106
  and Abraham Baldwin 105, 105, 106
  Constitutional Convention (1787) 104–106
  preamble to the **106**
  ratification of 106, 108, 111c
  and slavery 104–105
U.S. House of Representatives 105–106
U.S. Senate 105

V

Vatican, Rome 21
vegetable gardens 40
Verrazano, Giovanni da 2, 16
Vikings xiii, xiv
villages, Native American 9, 10, 12
Virginia xviiim, 25
  anti-British sentiment in 72
  Battle of Yorktown 97
  John Cabot 2
  cash crops in **35**
  at Constitutional Convention 104
  goal to capture 94
  and indentured servants **52**
  population of, in 1760 47
  and the Stamp Act Congress **77**
  ties to England of 73

W

Wall of China **55**
Walton, George **92,** 110c
war debt 68–69, 71, 73, 75, 100–101
wards, city **40**
War of 1812 15
War of Independence. *See* American Revolution
War of Jenkins' Ear 57–62, **59,** 94, 110c
Warren, Georgius Marinus 37
warriors 9, **11**
wars 14–15, 18. *See also specific headings, e.g.:* French and Indian Wars
Washington, George
  crosses the Delaware River 92
  named head of Continental army 90
  and soldiers for Georgia 94
  and Anthony Wayne 97, 98
wattle (as building material) 9, 10
Wayne, Anthony 97, 97, 98
wealth and illegal trade 75
Wesley, Charles 47, 48, 49, **50**
Wesley, John 47–48, 48, **50**
Whitefield, George 47, 48, 50, **50**
"white town" 9
Whitney, Eli 108
wild turkeys 14
women
  Mary Bosomworth 38, 65, **65,** 66
  Nancy Hart 96, **96**
  roles of Native American 14
Woodward, Dr. Henry 25, **26,** 27
working class **52**
Wormsloe Historic Site 114
Wren, Christopher 40
Wright, James 72, 72, 73
  leaves Georgia 90
  petitions of 83, 84
  return of 95
  and Sons of Liberty **76**
  and Stamp Act 79, 110c

Y

Yamacraw Bluff 37–38, 40, **40,** 109c
Yamacraw Indians 38, 38
  location of 58m
  and James Edward Oglethorpe 38
  Tomochichi 39
  Toonahowi 39
Yamasee Indians 4
  map of, in Georgia 5m
  and Spanish settlers 14
  war with 28
yellow fever **43**
Yorktown, Battle of 97
Yuchi Indians 25

Z

Zubly, John J. 90, **90**